CABINETS AND FIRST MINISTERS

Published in association with the Centre for Canadian Studies at Mount Allison University. Information on the Canadian Democratic Audit project can be found at www.CanadianDemocraticAudit.ca.

Advisory Group

William Cross, Director (Mount Allison University)
R. Kenneth Carty (University of British Columbia)
Elisabeth Gidengil (McGill University)
Richard Sigurdson (University of Manitoba)
Frank Strain (Mount Allison University)
Michael Tucker (Mount Allison University)

Titles

CABINETS AND FIRST MINISTERS

Graham White

UBCPress

15 14 13 12 11 10 09 08 07 06 05   5 4 3 2 1

Printed in Canada on acid-free paper that is 100% post-consumer recycled, processed chlorine-free, and printed with vegetable-based, low-VOC inks.

Library and Archives Canada Cataloguing in Publication

White, Graham, 1948-
  Cabinets and first ministers / Graham White.

(Canadian democratic audit ; 7)
Includes bibliographical references and index.
ISBN 0-7748-1101-3 (set). – ISBN 0-7748-1158-7 (bound); ISBN 0-7748-1159-5 (pbk)

  1. Cabinet system – Canada. 2. Prime ministers – Canada. 3. Cabinet ministers – Canada. 4. Power (Social sciences) – Canada. I. Title. II. Series.

JL97.W55 2005   321.8'043'0971   C2005-901099-1

Canadä

UBC Press gratefully acknowledges the financial support for our publishing program of the Government of Canada through the Book Publishing Industry Development Program (BPIDP), and of the Canada Council for the Arts and the British Columbia Arts Council.

The Centre for Canadian Studies thanks the Harold Crabtree Foundation for its support of the Canadian Democratic Audit project.

Printed and bound in Canada by Friesens.
Copy editor: Sarah Wight
Text design: Peter Ross, Counterpunch
Typesetter: Artegraphica Design Co. Ltd.
Proofreader: James Leahy
Indexer: Noeline Bridge

UBC Press
The University of British Columbia
2029 West Mall
Vancouver, BC V6T 1Z2
604-822-5959 / Fax: 604-822-6083
www.ubcpress.ca

For Cathy, Kate, Heather, and Patrick.
Mere words are so inadequate.

Contents

Tables

Foreword

This volume is part of the Canadian Democratic Audit series. The objective of this series is to consider how well Canadian democracy is performing at the outset of the twenty-first century. In recent years, political and opinion leaders, government commissions, academics, citizen groups, and the popular press have all identified a "democratic deficit" and "democratic malaise" in Canada. These characterizations often are portrayed as the result of a substantial decline in Canadians' confidence in their democratic practices and institutions. Indeed, Canadians are voting in record low numbers, many are turning away from the traditional political institutions, and a large number are expressing declining confidence in both their elected politicians and the electoral process.

Nonetheless, Canadian democracy continues to be the envy of much of the rest of the world. Living in a relatively wealthy and peaceful society, Canadians hold regular elections in which millions cast ballots. These elections are largely fair, efficient, and orderly events. They routinely result in the selection of a government with no question about its legitimate right to govern. Developing democracies from around the globe continue to look to Canadian experts for guidance in establishing electoral practices and democratic institutions. Without a doubt, Canada is widely seen as a leading example of successful democratic practice.

Given these apparently competing views, the time is right for a comprehensive examination of the state of Canadian democracy. Our purposes are to conduct a systematic review of the operations of Canadian democracy, to listen to what others have to say about Canadian democracy, to assess its strengths and weaknesses, to consider where there are opportunities for advancement, and to evaluate popular reform proposals.

A democratic audit requires the setting of benchmarks for evaluation of the practices and institutions to be considered. This necessarily involves substantial consideration of the meaning of democracy.

"Democracy" is a contested term and we are not interested here in striking a definitive definition. Nor are we interested in a theoretical model applicable to all parts of the world. Rather we are interested in identifying democratic benchmarks relevant to Canada in the twenty-first century. In selecting these we were guided by the issues raised in the current literature on Canadian democratic practice and by the concerns commonly raised by opinion leaders and found in public opinion data. We have settled on three benchmarks: public participation, inclusiveness, and responsiveness. We believe that any contemporary definition of Canadian democracy must include institutions and decision-making practices that are defined by public participation, that this participation must include all Canadians, and that government outcomes must respond to the views of Canadians.

While settling on these guiding principles, we have not imposed a strict set of democratic criteria on all of the evaluations that together constitute the Audit. Rather, our approach allows the auditors wide latitude in their evaluations. While all auditors keep the benchmarks of participation, inclusiveness, and responsiveness central to their examinations, each adds additional criteria of particular importance to the subject he or she is considering. We believe this approach of identifying unifying themes, while allowing for divergent perspectives, enhances the project by capturing the robustness of the debate surrounding democratic norms and practices.

We decided at the outset to cover substantial ground and to do so in a relatively short period. These two considerations, coupled with a desire to respond to the most commonly raised criticisms of the contemporary practice of Canadian democracy, result in a series that focuses on public institutions, electoral practices, and new phenomena that are likely to affect democratic life significantly. The series includes volumes that examine key public decision-making bodies: legislatures, the courts, and cabinets and government. The structures of our democratic system are considered in volumes devoted to questions of federalism and the electoral system. The ways in which citizens participate in electoral politics and policy making are a crucial component of the project, and thus we include studies of interest groups and political parties. The desire and capacity of Canadians for meaningful participation in public life is also the subject of a volume. Finally, the challenges and opportunities raised by new communication technologies are also considered. The Audit does not include studies devoted to the status of particular groups of Canadians. Rather than separate out Aboriginals, women, new Canadians, and others, these groups are treated together with all Canadians throughout the Audit.

In all, this series includes nine volumes examining specific areas of Canadian democratic life. A tenth, synthetic volume provides an overall assessment and makes sense out of the different approaches and findings found in the rest of the series. Our examination is not exhaustive. Canadian democracy is a vibrant force, the status of which can never be fully captured at one time. Nonetheless the areas we consider involve many of the pressing issues currently facing democracy in Canada. We do not expect to have the final word on this subject. Rather, we hope to encourage others to pursue similar avenues of inquiry.

A project of this scope cannot be accomplished without the support of many individuals. At the top of the list of those deserving credit are the members of the Canadian Democratic Audit team. From the very beginning, the Audit has been a team effort. This outstanding group of academics has spent many hours together, defining the scope of the project, prodding each other on questions of Canadian democracy, and most importantly, supporting one another throughout the endeavour, all with good humour. To Darin Barney, André Blais, Kenneth Carty, John Courtney, David Docherty, Joanna Everitt, Elisabeth Gidengil, Ian Greene, Richard Nadeau, Neil Nevitte, Richard Sigurdson, Jennifer Smith, Frank Strain, Michael Tucker, Graham White, and Lisa Young I am forever grateful.

The Centre for Canadian Studies at Mount Allison University has been my intellectual home for several years. The Centre, along with the Harold Crabtree Foundation, has provided the necessary funding and other assistance necessary to see this project through to fruition. At Mount Allison University, Peter Ennals provided important support to this project when others were skeptical; Wayne MacKay and Michael

Fox have continued this support since their respective arrivals on campus; and Joanne Goodrich and Peter Loewen have provided important technical and administrative help.

The University of British Columbia Press, particularly its senior acquisitions editor, Emily Andrew, has been a partner in this project from the very beginning. Emily has been involved in every important decision and has done much to improve the result. Camilla Blakeley has overseen the copyediting and production process and in doing so has made these books better. Scores of Canadian and international political scientists have participated in the project as commentators at our public conferences, as critics at our private meetings, as providers of quiet advice, and as referees of the volumes. The list is too long to name them all, but David Cameron, Sid Noel, Leslie Seidle, Jim Bickerton, Alexandra Dobrowolsky, Livianna Tossutti, Janice Gross Stein, and Frances Abele all deserve special recognition for their contributions. We are also grateful to the Canadian Study of Parliament Group, which partnered with us for our inaugural conference in Ottawa in November 2001.

Finally, this series is dedicated to all of the men and women who contribute to the practice of Canadian democracy. Whether as active participants in parties, groups, courts, or legislatures, or in the media and the universities, without them Canadian democracy would not survive.

William Cross
Director, The Canadian Democratic Audit
Sackville, New Brunswick

Acknowledgments

This book would not have been possible without the assistance and support of a great many people. First and foremost are Bill Cross and Emily Andrew. Bill's vision and energy in creating the Canadian Democratic Audit and seeing it through to fruition have been nothing short of remarkable; I was honoured (and more than a little daunted) when he asked me to contribute this volume to the series. Emily Andrew is surely the model of a university press editor: she facilitates, encourages, and advises, but she also reads manuscripts with care and insight, making valuable suggestions for improvement. My only complaint was Bill and Emily's non-negotiable insistence that no endnotes or footnotes would be allowed; for someone much given to tangents, this was a terrible restriction, but in the end I managed to produce an entire manuscript completely bereft of notes.[1]

My fellow authors on the Democratic Audit team proved admirable colleagues, sharing information and ideas generously and commenting on especially problematic sections of the manuscript constructively and quickly. Camilla Blakeley's smooth professionalism has once again contributed significantly to improving the book. Sarah Wight worked wonders polishing and reorganizing my oftentimes over-the-top prose. The two anonymous referees caught errors and, more significantly, provided me with many suggestions for improvements, almost all of which I accepted and incorporated into the final version of the book. Peter Aucoin, who rightly pushed me to fundamentally reframe the argument in Chapter 1, graciously shed his anonymity and reread the first chapter. Tom Mitchison, late of the Ontario Information and Privacy Commission, guided me through the intricacies of FOI legislation, but bears no responsibility for what I wrote in Chapter 4. Evert Lindquist offered many helpful comments on early phases of this project.

---

1 Almost.

Cabinet secretaries and their staffs across Canada were helpful in answering my questionnaire on various aspects of cabinet structure and process, and in some cases responding to follow-up e-mails and phone calls. Thanks are also due to the many ministers, bureaucrats, and politicos who agreed to not-for-attribution interviews as part of my ongoing research into Canadian core executives. Special thanks to the former premiers who permitted me to quote them directly in Chapter 3. I also want to record my thanks to the Social Sciences and Humanities Research Council of Canada, which funded the earlier cabinet research.

Gina Cosentino provided formidable research assistance, responding quickly and thoroughly to my most arcane and ill-defined requests for information and materials.

Those to whom I owe the greatest debt in completing this book haven't even read it: the love and support Cathy, Kate, Heather, and Patrick provide have been indispensable.

CABINETS AND FIRST MINISTERS

THE SCOPE AND CRITERIA FOR THE AUDIT

1

If asked which elements of their political system embody and safe-guard the democratic principles they hold dear, Canadians would doubtless mention elections, the media, political parties, and commu-nications with their elected representatives. Some would mention interest groups, social movements, street demonstrations, and the like; a few would even cite Parliament, the provincial and territorial legislatures, and possibly the courts. Only the most ingenuous – or those inclined to mischievous answers – might imagine that Canadian cabinets are in the least democratic.

Certainly, massive concentration of power is a defining feature of cabinets in Westminster-style political systems such as Canada's. Moreover, even in comparison with other Westminster systems, Cana-dian cabinets are notable for being dominated by their first ministers. Canadian cabinets, in other words, seem the very antithesis of democ-racy. Indeed, many blame Canadian democracy's most serious short-comings on the scarcely bridled power of the prime minister and the cabinet.

One response promoted by this line of thought is resigned realism: in any complex modern political system, democracy can only be about the processes for selecting and replacing leaders and the methods and institutions for holding them accountable. Ultimately, in Canada and elsewhere, once democratically selected, and subject to periodic accountability checks, top governmental decision makers wield extensive power with little pretence of democracy, at least in the short term. A less complacent approach holds that if decision making at Canada's highest governmental levels is fundamentally undemocratic, then the processes on which we stake our claim to be a democratic political system – including voting and elections, participation in interest groups and political parties, and various forms of political mobilization – are severely undercut.

Both responses rest on the accuracy of the initial premise: that Canadian cabinets are indeed highly undemocratic, with the corollary that significant change is unlikely or perhaps impossible. Yet democracy is not an either/or proposition; it is a matter of degree. No one would argue that the central decision-making processes of Canadian government are, or could be, democratic in the same ways that elections, methods of party leadership selection, or open municipal council meetings can be. Nonetheless, cabinets can be organized and can operate in ways that either diminish or enhance democracy. With cabinet's power and importance so far-reaching, even small democratic improvements or reversals are worth knowing about and worth analyzing. Moreover, while those with a vested interest in maintaining the status quo may not admit it, the reform possibilities are substantial and need not entail any heretical or radical deviation from the existing constitutional order. As one authority has written, "Without altering one iota of the constitutional conventions that give them their central energizing force, cabinets can operate in vastly different ways" (Dupré 1985, 3).

In short, including central executive structures and processes – primarily but not exclusively first ministers and cabinets – in the Democratic Audit of Canadian government and politics is not only appropriate but essential. We cannot simply describe our system as an elected dictatorship in which every three or four years the voters choose the top decision makers, who wield enormous power in a fundamentally undemocratic way until the next election. This view certainly has some truth to it, but the reality is a good deal more complex and may just allow for at least a modicum of democracy in the workings of cabinet. Moreover, the Democratic Audit, like conventional financial audits, can not only provide an assessment of current conditions but also point the way to realistic proposals for improvement. And few would disagree that improvement is needed.

Hence this book brings the Democratic Audit perspective to bear on the central mechanisms of Canadian government. The approach here is neither naïve nor fatalistic. Rather than making assumptions about the undemocratic nature of Canadian governmental structures and processes, this book asks questions about them, including questions about how they might be rendered more democratic.

Before proceeding too far down this road, let us ask some questions that might appear indelicate in a major project aiming at evaluating and improving democracy in Canada: How democratic do we want cabinet to be? Why should cabinet be democratic? The measure of the untoward concentration of power in the prime minister is said to be the relegation of cabinet to the status of focus group for the prime minister (Savoie 1999), but what's wrong with focus groups?

Cabinet is, after all, the principal executive body in Canadian government. In any organization, let alone one as mammoth as the federal government, the executive's function is to lead, to make decisions, and to implement policies. In a democratic system, the executive is expected to carry out its functions within a framework imbued with democratic values, but ultimately it has the authority — indeed the responsibility — to take and implement decisions without constantly returning to first democratic principles and processes. Overall, we should expect the governmental system to be democratic, but not all parts all the time (no one would propose that judges commission polls or hold town hall meetings on important or controversial cases). Parliament's lack of capacity to scrutinize or control cabinet may be cause for concern about the health of our democracy, but, as an executive body, cabinet cannot be held to the standards of a legislature. Simply put, cabinet's job is to take decisions. As the head of a democratically chosen government, it has a duty to render decisions and set priorities expeditiously — although not capriciously or arbitrarily — in order that government is able to respond effectively to public wants and demands.

This is not to argue that a simple trade-off exists between efficiency and democracy, for accepting such a calculus starts one down a very slippery slope indeed. Still, the danger is that the need to make a great many decisions, and some quite quickly, is not conducive to making them in as democratic a manner as possible.

Moreover, in the Canadian political system cabinet is multifunctional: it does a good deal more than make decisions. Among other things, cabinet scans the political, social, and economic environment for trends and problems; it monitors government and its effectiveness; it engages in strategic planning; it sets the political agenda; it serves important symbolic purposes; it combats the powerful centripetal forces in Canadian society; it promotes the inclusion of regional interests, and those of other social groupings, into the central processes of Canadian government; it gives leadership both in government and in society; and, as focus group, it advises the first minister. Thus judging cabinet and cabinet democracy solely by how decisions are made constitutes too narrow an approach.

How Democratic Can a Cabinet Be?

For all this, few would argue that Canadian cabinets are hamstrung by too much democracy. As executive bodies, are cabinets inherently and necessarily undemocratic?

The answer depends on what we mean by democracy. On the most basic level, democracy – literally, "rule by the people" – is straightforward. Rendering this abstract notion into more concrete terms applicable to modern-day Canadian politics, however, brings out the often disparate understandings of democracy. Indeed, it is telling that few serious analyses of democracy proceed very far before the adjectives begin to appear: not just "democracy," but direct democracy, social democracy, representative democracy, liberal democracy, and so on. Most descriptions of, or prescriptions for, democracy in Canada fall into one of three broad schools of thought, which share many assumptions while differing in important ways. Advocates of the three schools would evaluate both the democratic potential and the reality of cabinet quite differently. (The following discussion draws on Cameron, Mulhern, and White 2003.) These three principal strands of democratic practice and promise are representative democracy, direct democracy, and deliberative democracy.

REPRESENTATIVE DEMOCRACY

Probably the concept of democracy most familiar to Canadians, representative democracy is built on the premise that the people elect representatives to act on their behalf in formal government institutions. Citizens delegate extensive powers to these political elites. The House of Commons, provincial and territorial legislatures, and municipal councils are obvious and important illustrations of representative institutions embodying this understanding of democracy.

Important subsidiary principles underpin the basic conception of representative democracy, though substantial variations are possible in their practical realization (for example, representatives may be elected by proportional representation or by the first-past-the-post system; see Courtney 2004). Representatives must be chosen through free and fair electoral processes. Formal mechanisms must be in place to ensure the accountability of elected representatives and the transparency of their actions. A balance must be struck between the imperatives of majority rule and the protection of minority rights. Respect for the rule of law and for due process must inform governance.

DIRECT DEMOCRACY

Direct democracy is rooted in a populist suspicion of elite-dominated representative institutions, which are seen as susceptible to losing touch with the voters who elected them. In order to ensure that governments are responsive and accountable to the people, they must be subject to direct control by the people. For advocates of direct democracy, "The very essence of democracy lies in recognizing that sovereignty rests with all citizens rather than exclusively with a small group of representatives, no matter how carefully chosen" (LeDuc 2003, 40-1). Political elites must therefore be constrained to act in accord with public opinion. This entails curtailing their discretion, so that elected officials behave as delegates, who follow their constituents' directions, rather than as representatives, who exercise their own best judgment. Such mechanisms as recall, referendum, initiative (whereby citizens can launch policy proposals into the formal legislative process), and term limits give voters direct control over their elected representatives and over the outcome of specific policy issues. For reasons we cannot explore here, enthusiasm for direct democracy has been strongest in Western Canada.

Direct democracy processes have a black-and-white character to them – yes or no on a referendum question, for example – reflecting a belief that even apparently complex problems ultimately have simple solutions. This is linked to the principle that democracy is served when a clear, direct expression of the public will (i.e., a vote) binds public officials to a certain course of action, effectively settling the issue without need for further deliberation or opportunity for revision. A related notion is faith in the common sense of the common people, which translates into distrust of experts and unelected, unaccountable public servants, be they government bureaucrats, academics, or judges.

DELIBERATIVE DEMOCRACY

The term "deliberative democracy" has emerged only in the past two decades, but the essential ideas underpinning it are of long standing. Elements of what would now be seen as deliberative democracy may be found in ancient Athenian assemblies, New England town hall meetings, and ideas about so-called participatory democracy in the 1960s. The consensus style of decision making found in some Aboriginal societies has strong echoes of deliberative democracy.

The central tenet of deliberative democracy holds that decisions are best reached through public deliberation – argument, debate, exchange of ideas – among citizens: "talk-centric democratic theory replaces vote-centric democratic theory" (Chambers 2003, 308). The expectation is not that in real-world situations every person would participate actively and extensively. Rather, deliberative democracy envisions public forums to which the entire citizenry has equal access and thus equal opportunity to participate, even if most do not, indeed cannot, take it up. A wide range of views are expressed and discussed in these forums. Both active participants and passive members of the audience (who are nonetheless attentive and engaged) are sufficiently open-minded to revise their views in response to the discussion. The process of deliberation and decision making becomes intertwined with the outcome; or, as a pair of writers summarizes a prominent strand of theorizing about deliberative democracy, the "transformative power of politics makes democratic engagement an end in itself; deliberative democracy should be advocated precisely because of the beneficial educative effects it has on citizens" (Bohman and Rehg 1997, xii). Real-life institutions embodying deliberative democracy principles include citizen/constituent assemblies, citizen juries, and certain forms of commissions of inquiry (for example, those with intervenor funding).

CABINET'S ROLE IN A REPRESENTATIVE DEMOCRACY

Elements of direct democracy – occasional plebiscites and referenda – and of deliberative democracy – British Columbia's citizen assembly on electoral reform and Ontario's citizen juries – are emerging in Canada. Even if such practices become more common, however, representative institutions and processes will remain the principal means by which Canadians practise democracy.

Accordingly, to return to the question of whether cabinet is inherently undemocratic, the recognition that Canada is and will remain a representative democracy provides the answer. Cabinet is part and parcel of the system of representative institutions and responsible government that constitute Canadian democracy. Those who advocate the application of the norms and expectations of direct and deliberative democracy to Canadian core executives will surely be disappointed and conclude that Canadian cabinets and the system of responsible government that underpins them are undemocratic. Such standards, however, are largely unrealistic and inappropriate. Cabinet is drawn from and is responsible to the elected representatives in our parliaments and legislatures. This book is premised on the assumption that cabinets can be organized and can operate in ways that enhance or diminish democracy, but the elemental fact is that executives in democratic systems are democratic institutions.

Over a century ago, the great constitutional scholar A.V. Dicey, who embodied conservative, traditional thinking about British-style political institutions, had this to say about the constitutional conventions of the Westminster system: "They have all one ultimate objective. Their end is to secure that Parliament, or the Cabinet which is indirectly appointed by Parliament, shall in the long run give effect to the will of that power which in modern England is the true political sovereign of the State – the majority of the electors" (Dicey [1885] 1956, 429). The language may be dated but the message is clear, and all the more convincing given the often narrow ideas about democracy in Dicey's era: cabinet is an integral component of our representative democracy.

The concentration of power that is said to increasingly characterize cabinets (or more accurately, their first ministers) may well constitute a significant diminution of democracy. Indeed for that reason this issue is examined at some length in this book. The mere fact that first ministers and their cabinets possess substantial executive power, however, is not inherently undemocratic.

The Comparative Context of the Audit

Auditing cabinet democracy in Canada necessarily involves more than an examination of decision making in Ottawa. Provinces and territories play a prominent role in the governance of Canadians, ranking as they do among the most powerful subnational governments in the world. Moreover, not only are provincial and territorial cabinets worth evaluating as important players in critical democratic processes, but incorporating them into the study substantially enhances its analytical possibilities. The analysis is thus at once prompted and facilitated by comparative analysis.

In general, provincial cabinets conform to the variation of the Westminster model dominant in Ottawa, but they are scarcely uniform. The differences they exhibit – both from the federal cabinet and among themselves – offer additional scope for addressing issues of cabinet democracy. Typically, for example, they are smaller, less institutionalized, and have call on central agencies with fewer resources than does the national cabinet, though in important respects cabinets in the largest provinces more closely resemble the federal cabinet than they do their counterparts in the smallest provinces.

While the territories' minuscule populations severely limit their significance in any national sense, their governments exercise almost all of the main powers of provinces and, given the critical role of the public sector in the far North, they play especially large roles in the lives of northern residents. But territorial cabinets are worth including in the democratic audit not simply by virtue of their local importance. The so-called consensus governments in Nunavut and the Northwest Territories – in essence Westminster cabinet-parliamentary systems without political parties – demonstrate the possibility of organizing cabinet government along lines quite different from those operative in Ottawa and the provincial capitals.

In addition, though this is not a book on international issues of cabinet organization and process, the problems and prospects of the Canadian core executive are hardly unique to this country. Accordingly, comparisons and insights are drawn from the Anglo-Celtic democracies rooted in the Westminster model.

Cabinet Principles: Responsible Government and Democracy

Before setting out the audit criteria that guide the analysis, it will be useful to examine whether a "democratic deficit" indeed exists in Canada in terms of the links between cabinet government and democracy. Is the system of responsible government as practised in Canada, also known as the Westminster system after the London district containing the British Parliament, rooted in fundamentally democratic precepts? Has there been a failure to realize the system's inherently democratic character, or have democratic impulses been unable to alter the system's fundamentally undemocratic core significantly? A summary of the principles of responsible government will help answer these questions.

Responsible government cannot be put to a democratic litmus test in an analytical vacuum. Short of outright dictatorships, all systems of governance have both democratic and undemocratic features. Accordingly, when we are totting up the democratic pluses and minuses of responsible government it should be understood that without an explicit comparative framework that considers warts-and-all portraits of alternative systems, we must be leery of drawing conclusions about Canada's cabinet-parliamentary system. Simplistic overgeneralizations are not helpful. Still, as the core of Canadian governance, responsible government must be assessed for its democratic strengths and weaknesses.

Clearly, certain cardinal principles on which Canadian cabinets are predicated run directly counter to democratic precepts. Cabinet was never intended to be democratic. On the contrary, the institution took shape long before current notions of democracy emerged, and it developed as a vehicle for the exercise of power beyond popular control or consent. Although cabinet has adapted in important ways to democratic imperatives, its antidemocratic roots run deep.

Cabinet's historical antecedents lie in the institutionalization of the king's private circle of advisors in the seventeenth century. To this day the constitutional theory underpinning Canadian government holds that the authority exercised by cabinet has been delegated downward from the monarch rather than upward from the people and their elected representatives in Parliament. Even the basic tenets of responsible government, which subject the power of cabinet to the consent of elected parliamentarians, largely predate the democratic era. (In Canada, as in Britain, parliamentary elections tended to be an elite preserve until at least the 1860s, by which time responsible government as we now know it was firmly established.) Responsible government and the privileged place of cabinet within it was rooted in the strong deference to authority that characterized British and Canadian politics in the nineteenth century. Canadian society may have experienced a marked "decline of deference" in recent years (Nevitte 1996), but its most powerful political institutions continue to reflect the mindset of the nineteenth century.

The four central principles of responsible government that follow must be examined with respect to their democratic disposition:

1   cabinet's monopoly on executive power
2   the requirement for cabinet to be responsible to the House, in the sense of maintaining its confidence
3   the collective nature of cabinet, or cabinet solidarity
4   ministerial responsibility.

Important variations in political practices are evident across Canada's provincial, territorial, and national governments (as across the Anglo-Celtic democracies), but all adhere to these same constitutional principles. These principles do *not* hold sway at the municipal level; linkages between the executives and the legislatures of even Canada's largest cities are based on very different principles and hence are not examined in this book.

Westminster cabinets wield sweeping executive powers, reflecting their predemocratic origins as agents of the monarch's authority. This is evident in their absolute control over the bureaucratic apparatus of the state: although the democratically elected Parliament can call public servants to account, control and direction of the bureaucracy is entirely a cabinet prerogative. An even more telling illustration is the constitutional restriction on who may impose taxes and spend public money. While cabinet requires parliamentary authorization to tax or spend, only ministers are constitutionally entitled to *propose* such measures in Parliament; private members of Parliament – nonministers – are not even permitted to initiate so-called money bills or amendments. Additionally, through the use of regulations and similar legal instruments, vast swaths of government activity can be authorized and implemented by what amounts to cabinet decree with no need for parliamentary approval and precious little parliamentary scrutiny.

Perhaps the most basic element of responsible government stipulates that the cabinet gains and holds power by maintaining the support of a majority of the members of the House of Commons (or legislature), as manifested by winning all the crucial votes. This confidence convention does not, as is often thought, mean that any government defeat is cause for an election or for the government to resign. Only on basic elements of government policy, most notably the Throne Speech and the budget (the overall budget, not individual spending or taxing measures), or on motions explicitly designated as confidence matters, do defeats in Parliament threaten the life of the government. In this important way, Canadian government is characterized by a constitutional separation of legislature (Parliament) and executive (cabinet) (Aucoin 1999, 109).

This central precept was not designed to be democratic. (Of course, no aspects of responsible government were consciously *designed* by anyone; they simply emerged over time.) As the House of Commons came to be elected by universal suffrage, however (universal male suffrage until the twentieth century), the confidence requirement took on a decidedly democratic bent, with cabinet power resting on the consent of the people's elected representatives. (Significantly, the appointed Senate, like the House of Lords in Britain, has never played a role in confidence questions.) The constitutional convention requiring ministers to hold seats in Parliament, explored in Chapter 2, is inherently democratic not only in ensuring that ministers are themselves directly subject to the popular will by obligating them to seek election and re-election but also in compelling their regular presence among the elected representatives. (Constitutional conventions are binding rules governing the operation of the political system which are not formalized in writing and hence are not legally enforceable by the courts [Heard 1991].)

This sounds wonderfully democratic but has more than a little air of unreality. Constitutional theory may be couched in terms of the separation of legislative and executive functions, and cabinet's subjugation to Parliament, but political reality is very different. In political terms, the hallmark of the Westminster system is a virtual fusion of executive and legislative power and overwhelming cabinet dominance. The vehicle for imposing and maintaining this dominance is party discipline.

Party discipline is examined in *Legislatures*, David Docherty's (2004) democratic audit of Parliament and legislatures. For present purposes we need recognize only that while the theory of responsible government is oblivious to political parties and party discipline, the real-life operation of our cabinet-parliamentary system is literally incomprehensible without them. (Note that responsible government itself does not require political parties, as shown by the legislatures of Nunavut and the Northwest Territories.) The unusually strong party discipline evident in Canada's Parliament and legislatures (working in concert with an electoral system that typically produces clear majority governments even in the absence of majority electoral support for the victorious party) effectively gives Canadian cabinets all but unshakeable control over the House of Commons and its provincial counterparts.

The third responsible government principle ensures that cabinet government is very much collective government. Unity is more than a strategy for political survival, reflecting the maxim that those who do not hang together will surely hang separately; it is constitutionally required in Westminster systems. (Some experts see cabinet solidarity as a political convention rather than a constitutional principle, but no one disputes its importance.) The doctrine of cabinet solidarity requires ministers to uphold cabinet decisions and government policy regardless of their personal views. Ministers may vigorously oppose a proposal during cabinet deliberations, but once the decision is taken, they must support it in public and take responsibility for it. This principle both enhances and undermines democracy. By clearly identifying ultimate responsibility for critical government decisions, and thereby offering the public the opportunity to punish or reward those responsible at election time, it establishes strong democratic accountability. At the same time, artificial unity where division exists beneath the surface and the curtailment of the public airing of differences within cabinet reduce the ability of citizens and groups to identify possible cabinet allies and to press their opposition to policies.

The ministerial responsibility principle requires ministers to be not only collectively responsible for government decisions but also individually responsible for their departments. The practical import is that elected ministers rather than appointed bureaucrats answer for the conduct of public affairs. This is essential if the political neutrality of the public service is to be maintained. Again, however, insistence on individual ministerial responsibility entails pluses and minuses for democracy. Clear identification of a single responsible figure – the minister – promotes democratic accountability. As well, many would see a politically neutral bureaucracy as essential to a healthy democracy. Conversely, democracy may not be served when the bureaucrats actually responsible for much of what government does are absolved from public accountability for their actions and omissions. A contrary view of the merits of a politically neutral public service exists, at least with respect to the higher echelons of the bureaucracy. To establish and implement its policies effectively, this argument runs, a political party requires politically engaged and supportive senior public servants, especially if the party intends significant change.

Finally, a quirk in how individual ministerial responsibility plays out in Parliament undercuts democracy. Ministers are responsible for their current, but not their former, departments; while this reflects a certain logic, ensuring that someone is always responsible, it also enables ministers to evade accountability. The current minister must accept formal responsibility, but this is often inadequate when problems were clearly the former minister's doing.

In looking at the principles that underlie cabinet government in Canada, we must distinguish the fundamental imperatives of responsible government, with their essential constitutional character, from the political practices that have emerged in Canadian cabinet construction and operation. The latter, while crucial for understanding and evaluating cabinets, could be altered without challenging the essential nature of the system. Such a fundamental challenge may well be warranted, but would go beyond the scope of the current exercise; audits seek to improve existing systems, not replace them. This distinction can be illustrated by contrasting the four central constitutional precepts discussed above with important, long-standing Canadian political practices, such as the rarity of coalition cabinets, and the construction of cabinets so as to give voice to regions and groups.

So, *is* responsible government democratic? Important historical antecedents of modern-day Westminster cabinets, some of which continue to shape governmental processes, were decidedly undemocratic. Yet responsible government is ultimately representative government and thus firmly democratic. The (allegedly) growing concentration of power in the core executive, which rightly excites concern about the erosion of democracy by excluding most of the people's representatives from wielding real influence, smacks of a throwback to the predemocratic roots of Westminster cabinets. While indeed worrisome, this trend is not intrinsic to responsible government. British-style responsible government can and should be an effective means of realizing representative government. The question of course is whether, as practised in Canada, this potential is being fulfilled. The nature and operation of cabinet and core executive figure prominently in answering this question.

The Audit Target: Cabinet and Core Executive

Before proceeding further, it behooves us to clarify just what is being audited in this book. Though cabinet is the central focus of attention, we employ an expansive understanding of the term, encompassing rather more than simply the collection of ministers who gather regularly around the cabinet table. Let us briefly consider the notion of cabinet.

In government circles the term "the centre" has gained wide currency. Academics have also adopted the term: Donald Savoie's influential book (1999) lamenting the decline of cabinet is titled *Governing from the centre.* Though the centre is not always defined with precision, it is clearly not synonymous with cabinet but also encompasses the central political and bureaucratic agencies such as the Privy Council Office and the Prime Minister's Office. Savoie's analysis explicitly links the centre with the subordination of cabinet to the prime minister and his or her political-bureaucratic support system; others implicitly make similar assumptions.

Rather than proceeding from the postulate that the centre has eclipsed the cabinet as the prime locus of power, this book employs a broad concept of central governance institutions, in which cabinet is an important, but by no means the only, player. British scholars writing about cabinet and the web of institutions and relations in which it is embedded have come to favour the notion of "core executive" as more accurately capturing the breadth and complexity of the central institutions of modern governance. R.A.W. Rhodes defines the core executive as "all those organisations and procedures which coordinate central government policies, and act as final arbiters of conflict between different parts of the government machine" (Rhodes 1995, 12). The core executive in Canada entails cabinet, the central agencies, and related supporting institutions and personnel, such as ministerial political staff and deputy ministers of line departments. This is a somewhat wider notion than Savoie's centre, which does not include either line deputies or ministers' political staff. Another difference is that the core executive concept is less determinist about the role and nature of cabinet. Just as powerful central agencies, beholden to the prime minister, may diminish cabinet's influence, so too, other elements, such as ministers' personal staffs, may enhance cabinet power.

For all this, cabinet remains the core of the core executive. Yet when we address the extent of cabinet democracy and the possibilities for enhancing it, two different approaches, and the concerns that arise from them, must be kept analytically distinct. Essentially, the distinction is between cabinet as a unitary actor atop the government decision-making structure and cabinet as a complex, internally differentiated institution in its own right. Unless this distinction between cabinet's external and internal relationships is made explicit, confusion about the concentration of power at the centre and about cabinets and democracy is likely.

The first approach, which sees cabinet as one part of a larger entity, doesn't ask how cabinet decisions are reached but focuses instead on the role cabinet (including the first minister) collectively plays within the governmental system: Who has the opportunity to present requests and recommendations to cabinet? Who has influence over cabinet? Are there countervailing sites of power and influence that limit cabinet's capacity to act? Are cabinet decisions implemented without question or interference? Are there effective mechanisms for scrutiny and control of cabinet? In other words, does cabinet wield unbridled and undemocratic power in setting public policy? This perspective leads to questions such as those raised by Savoie in his warning about the untoward concentration of power at the centre. Yet questions pointing in another direction are also possible. For example, the "hollowing out of the state" thesis argues that the capacity of the state to take authoritative action in its traditional realms of activity is being progressively undermined by a powerful constellation of secular forces. These include the increasing power of complex webs of interest groups, the shift away from traditional governmental structures to new modes of governance such as privatization, alternate service delivery mechanisms, special operating agencies, and the like, and the growing constraints on the capacity of the nation-state represented by transnational economic and political institutions (Weller, Bakvis, and Rhodes 1997).

The second approach to cabinet derives from the recognition that, while it often seems an undifferentiated monolith, in reality cabinet is a complex institution with its own internal power configurations and decision-making processes. Perhaps the most crucial question from this perspective is the role and influence of the first minister, though many others bear investigation. For example, how do the formal and informal hierarchies of ministers affect individual ministers' capacity to bring their views forward? Does extensive recourse to cabinet committees make for greater diffusion of power in cabinet decision making? To what extent does ministers' influence over cabinet decisions reflect the sociodemographic groups that they are seen to represent?

In short, one set of questions asks about the democratic implications of cabinet's position within the governmental system and the other is concerned with the nature of internal cabinet processes. Ultimately, of course, cabinet's control over government and public policy is linked to its internal organization and operation, but in our democratic audit of Canadian core executives, these elements of governance are kept separate.

The Audit Criteria

As a central institution in our system of representative, responsible government, cabinet is, as discussed above, a democratic institution. Democratic considerations, however, are not usually seen to figure prominently in the organization and operation of Canada's core executives. On the surface the key benchmarks of the Democratic Audit – public participation, responsiveness, and inclusiveness – seem inappropriate. They can nevertheless be refined so that they may be sensibly applied to core executives. In addition, the supplementary criteria of accountability and transparency, often cited as key to effective democracy, warrant special attention as regards government decision making.

Public Participation

Public participation in cabinet and other core executive activities is virtually nil, but if we bear in mind that cabinet is part of a system of representative democratic institutions and modify the notion to incorporate participation by the representatives of the public, rather more interesting possibilities arise.

Before turning to them, however, let us not completely dismiss direct public participation. Cabinets or cabinet committees may permit organizations or even individuals to meet with them, either on a routine (albeit infrequent) basis or in special circumstances. Cabinets and cabinet committees also travel outside the capital, sometimes to receive deputations from organized interests, sometimes to hear directly from individual citizens. It is worth exploring how common such occurrences may be and also how genuine they are: do they have any significant democratic value as participatory exercises or are they essentially hollow public relations charades? Rather less frequent and consequential are instances in which cabinet serves as the appeal body for decisions of adjudicative agencies. The democratic potential for citizens and groups to challenge administrative decisions through cabinet processes is obvious, but is it realized? These questions are examined in Chapter 4.

A focus on participation by the public's representatives in cabinet and cabinet processes suggests several sets of questions about who takes part in cabinet decision making. First and foremost is the question of the involvement and influence of cabinet ministers. At first blush, asking about ministers' participation in cabinet might seem passing strange – ministers *are* cabinet. Yet accounts of cabinet that emphasize the overwhelming dominance of the first minister and see cabinet as little more than a focus group for the prime minister (such as Savoie 1999) effectively argue that ministers' participation in cabinet is more ritualistic than substantive. A central issue in assessing Canadian democracy (let alone Canadian cabinets) is the degree to which power has been concentrated in the first minister to the exclusion of other elected officials, ministers included. Accordingly, Chapter 3 is devoted to evaluating the power of the first minister, especially vis-à-vis cabinet.

The question of ministerial participation in cabinet goes beyond issues of the first minister's dominance. Cabinet is nominally a collegial body in which – the first minister aside – ministers engage in genuinely collective decision making, with all participants possessing voice and influence. The reality is of course that like the denizens of Animal Farm, some ministers are more equal than others. Assessing democracy within cabinet thus entails study of the pecking order within cabinet. It also entails judgments about cabinet decision making: How much leeway have individual ministers to act independent of cabinet? Just how collective and collegial are cabinet processes? Are cabinets characterized by collective, collegial decision making more democratic than those in which important decisions are taken by individual ministers acting largely in isolation? (These questions are tied in to issues of cabinet organization and process, discussed below under responsiveness, and the subject of Chapter 5.)

Ministers are not the only representatives of the public who take part in cabinet decision making. Though private members of Parliament/legislatures clearly are not central players, they may also participate in cabinet processes. This participation takes two forms: individual private members attending and contributing to cabinet (or more likely, cabinet committee) meetings, and involvement in cabinet decisions by the government caucus. Typically such involvement comes after the fact, through caucus review or approval of cabinet decisions, but it may take the form of genuine participation prior to cabinet reaching a decision. The extent and effect of such practices are examined in Chapter 4.

RESPONSIVENESS

Responsiveness is primarily about taking action in accord with the wishes of the public: addressing issues that concern the population and adopting policies in accord with its wishes. Other authors in the Democratic Audit project refer to these as "democratic outcomes." Accountability and transparency are elements of this calculus but are treated separately below. Responsiveness also carries connotations of capacity to respond quickly, which are not directly relevant to democratic concerns.

For a variety of reasons, we cannot directly evaluate core executive responsiveness, or measure whether cabinet decisions are democratic outcomes. We can, however, consider some second-order indicators. The involvement of the government caucus, and to a lesser extent individual private members, in cabinet processes has a direct and obvious bearing on responsiveness. So, too, in a very limited way, cabinet's role as appeal body may be seen in terms of responsiveness.

More influential for responsiveness are issues of cabinet organization and process. These may seem mere plumbing – structural detail with little effect on substantive decisions – but how issues come before cabinet, what sort of information and analysis decisions are based on, and how cabinet deals with the business before it bear directly on responsiveness. As late as the 1970s some provincial cabinets lacked written agendas or formal minutes, but the "institutionalized cabinet" (Dupré 1985) has since become the norm. Core executives have adopted highly formal processes and routines and developed complex structures in the form of cabinet committee systems and support agencies. Is the result a boon or barrier to democracy? Does a formal, disciplined process for cabinet decision making increase or diminish the likelihood that important issues are accorded sufficient and informed attention by cabinet so that decisions are not taken precipitately or capriciously – and by extension unresponsively and undemocratically?

Assessment of responsiveness in the core executive cannot overlook the role of the senior bureaucracy, especially the powerful central agency bureaucrats. Do they subvert the will of the democratically elected political leadership? Are they gatekeepers who filter out ideas and proposals from ministers and line departments not to their liking, or even impose their own agendas? Or do they facilitate the flow of information and advice and assist ministers and their departments in navigating the shoals and reefs of cabinet decision making?

Political staff are also germane in assessments of cabinet responsiveness. Canadian cabinets are characterized by substantial numbers of partisan political staff, both in central agencies like the Prime Minister's Office and in individual ministers' offices. Since political staff often wield considerable clout, the question arises as to whether they contribute to or detract from democracy. Given their explicitly political mandate and orientation, do they promote stronger, more direct linkages with the people and serve as a counterweight to the unelected bureaucrats? Or, by facilitating access to political decision makers for those with party and political connections, do they constitute an undemocratic avenue of influence for a select few? All these aspects of responsiveness are addressed in Chapter 5.

INCLUSIVENESS

Cabinets surely rank among the most exclusive bodies in Canada, limited to twenty or thirty people, who gain admission and retain membership only with the first minister's approval. In literal terms, the discussion of cabinet inclusiveness is over before it begins. Again, though, an expansive rendering of the notion suggests more promising lines of inquiry.

One measure of inclusiveness is social diversity. For most of Canadian history, cabinets were anything but diverse, dominated as they were by middle-aged professional males of Anglo-Celtic or francophone heritage. In recent years, demographic and attitudinal transformations in Canadian society have been partially reflected in cabinet membership, rendering cabinets somewhat more diverse, and hence more inclusive, in their social composition. Cabinets necessarily reflect the membership of the legislatures from which they are drawn, however, and David Docherty's analysis in this series (2004) demonstrates that while some sociodemographic groups now have representation in Parliament that they lacked not so long ago, changes in the social composition of legislatures still lag well behind societal changes. And of course some groups are completely excluded: by definition there are no poor or unemployed MPs or ministers.

The extent to which cabinet mirrors the sociodemographic profile of the Canadian public is certainly significant, but rather more important are the potential implications for inclusiveness of what has been styled the "representational imperative." A defining feature of Canadian cabinets, this principle holds that so far as possible all regions as well as all important ethnic, cultural, and linguistic groups and various other politically salient groups (such as women and certain occupations) should be represented in cabinet by ministers sharing their sociodemographic characteristics. The effects of the representational imperative on decision making must be considered: How is the composition of cabinet linked to its operation? What role, for example, do regional ministers play? More generally, does ministerial influence within cabinet reflect representational considerations? Does having a regional or group representative at the cabinet table really constitute inclusiveness? And, harkening back to the point of the previous paragraph, can we really speak of inclusiveness when many interests and social groupings are not formally represented in cabinet? The representational imperative is discussed in Chapter 5.

ACCOUNTABILITY AND TRANSPARENCY

Clear, robust accountability is one of the great strengths of responsible government. At the same time, the Westminster system has long been notorious for its thoroughgoing lack of transparency: all the important decisions are made behind closed doors and cabinet secrecy is suffocatingly all-encompassing. (This is not to suggest that other forms of government are notably more open or transparent, though this intriguing question cannot be pursued in this book.)

Most of the crucial questions about core executive accountability fall under the rubric of parliamentary scrutiny and control of the government and are thus more fittingly discussed in David Docherty's democratic audit of Parliament, *Legislatures*. While not abandoning all concern with accountability, this volume will concentrate on the transparency of core executive processes. (One facet of cabinet accountability that will be explored relates to the accountability-averse realm of executive federalism.)

Traditionally, cabinet government was shrouded in secrecy: in Britain until the 1970s, even the existence and names of cabinet committees were considered state secrets (Hennessy 1986). Canadian cabinets are hardly paragons of open government, but in recent years court decisions, rulings from freedom of information commissions, and public inquiries have all breached the ramparts of cabinet secrecy by making public documents that not so long ago would have been embargoed for decades. The public has been able to gain limited access to key cabinet documents, submissions going before cabinet, and records of cabinet discussions and decisions. Chapter 4 considers whether these are isolated instances that do not fundamentally challenge the opaqueness of cabinet processes or prefigure a new era of transparency. In this light, British Columbia's experiment with "open cabinet," featuring such heretical practices as televising certain cabinet meetings and posting cabinet submissions on the Internet, is intriguing. Easily dismissed as completely bogus, open cabinet nonetheless warrants attention if only for the possibilities it presents.

Organization of the Book

In the foregoing discussion, many specific issues could have been addressed under two or more of the audit criteria. By way of illustration, evaluation of the first minister's power, framed as a participation issue, extends to the role of political staff and central agency bureaucrats, discussed under responsiveness. Similarly, questions arising from formal and informal division of cabinets into inner and outer tiers pertain to both participation and inclusiveness. The analysis in Chapters 4 and 5 takes a more integrative approach, recognizing that a practice or structure may have implications for more than one of the generic audit criteria.

The balance of the book is organized as follows. Chapter 2 is an overview of Canadian cabinets: their development, structure, and operation. This includes description and analysis of the principal components of

Canadian core executives, discussion of the similarities and differences among federal and provincial core executives, and a brief account of the unusual system of consensus government found in Nunavut and the Northwest Territories. Chapter 3 examines the notion that Canadian prime ministers and premiers and the political-bureaucratic apparatus surrounding them wield all but dictatorial powers. Chapters 4 and 5 examine the remaining topics mentioned above:

- public access to cabinet processes
- public access to cabinet documents
- cabinet as appeal body
- participation by private members in cabinet processes
- cabinet as collective, collegial body
- cabinet organization and processes
- the influence of central agency bureaucrats
- the influence of political staff
- the representational imperative
- executive federalism.

In Chapter 6, overall conclusions are drawn about core executives and democracy in Canada, and ideas are offered for possible reforms, drawing on both Canadian and international experiences. An appendix briefly sets out the sources employed to conduct the audit.

In looking at these various topics, the audit will attempt to provide explanation as well as evaluation. For example, the analysis will consider not just the extent of public access to cabinet processes and which forms of public access afford the best prospects for enhancing democracy, but why differences have emerged across jurisdictions. Variations within jurisdictions are also important. Core executive structures and processes are not static, nor are changes in them unidirectional. Participation and responsiveness, for example, may vary a good deal depending on the issue area and perhaps on the phase of budget cycle. The influence of central agency bureaucrats and the domination of the first minister may vary accordingly to how long a government or first minister has been in power.

CHAPTER 1

- ✚ British-style (Westminster) political systems are characterized by concentration of power in their executives: the first minister and the cabinet.

- ✚ Even by Westminster standards Canadian cabinets and first ministers possess unusual power.

- ✚ Elements of direct and deliberative democracy exist in Canada, but our system is essentially one of representative democracy.

- ✚ Despite the power they wield, Canadian cabinets are not inherently undemocratic; rather, they form an integral part of our representative democracy.

- ✚ In analyzing the central decision-making institutions of Canadian government, it is often useful to think in terms of the core executive rather than simply the first minister and cabinet.

- ✚ The democratic audit of cabinets and first ministers is premised on the recognition that core executive institutions can be organized in very different ways (all in keeping with Westminster constitutional principles), which can enhance or diminish democracy.

CABINET GOVERNMENT IN CANADA: AN EXECUTIVE SUMMARY

2

All but the most profoundly apolitical Canadian doubtless understands the primary elements of cabinet government: a small band of elected politicians, led by a dominating prime minister or premier, wields extensive decision-making power over government and public policy. Yet partly because of the aura of secrecy suffusing cabinets, even the most politically involved may not know a great deal more than that. Newly appointed ministers sometimes take up their posts largely ignorant of central features of cabinet structure and operation. Accordingly, before embarking on an audit of core executives in Canada, we need a clear appreciation of what cabinet is and how it works. This chapter therefore provides an overview of cabinet government, Canadian style, setting out the basic structural, historical, and operational aspects of Canadian core executives – federal, provincial, and territorial.

The phrase "cabinet government, Canadian style" is used advisedly since, although the purpose is not a broad comparative analysis, Canadian variations on the basic Westminster model are highlighted at various junctures. The aim is not to divine a coherent, uniquely Canadian model of cabinet but to recognize that departures from what might be seen as the norm may be appropriate and desirable. In part, then, this chapter lays the groundwork for recommendations in the final chapter that might seem at first blush to deviate from accepted cabinet ortho-doxy. When the conventional wisdom of just what cabinet government entails is closely examined, it becomes evident that – beyond empty formalities – no firm, enduring practical definition of cabinet govern-ment is possible. "There is," as one scholar puts it, "no such thing as a 'Westminster system' only a divergent and diverging family of govern-ments" (Rhodes 2000, 258). Cabinet government has always been some-thing of a moveable feast, a shifting set of arrangements that evolve to meet the economic and political pressures of the day (Weller 2003). As such, it is remarkably flexible and adaptable.

Central Characteristics of Canadian Cabinets

The principal elements of Canadian cabinets can be set out succinctly. Many of course are shared with cabinets in the other Anglo-Celtic democracies adhering to the classic Westminster model of cabinet-parliamentary government, but some are unique to Canada. Canadian cabinets tend to be powerful, secretive, bureaucratic bodies dominated by the first minister and composed of elected but often inexperi-enced legislators from the governing party, chosen in part for socio-demographic and regional diversity. These characteristics merit some discussion.

Canadian cabinets are very powerful. First ministers, the unelected political-bureaucratic apparatus around them, senior bureaucrats, well-connected interest groups, international economic organizations, transnational corporations, and others stand accused of usurping cab-inet's power. Still, Canadian cabinets unquestionably remain powerful: individual ministers can and do take far-reaching decisions within their departments, while cabinet collectively constitutes the central locus of governmental power in our system. Like most powerful bodies, and political executives in other forms of government, Canadian cabi-nets are also highly secretive. Unofficial leaks occur, often ministeri-ally sanctioned or instigated, but cabinet secrecy nonetheless enjoys the status of constitutional principle and access to cabinet documents is closely guarded.

Canadian cabinets are, by international standards, unusually large. The Alberta cabinet typically comprises more ministers than its counterparts in Britain or Australia. (The comparison is not exact; as discussed below, British ministries – which include cabinet and layers of junior ministers – can reach a hundred or more.) Most Canadian cabinets range between fifteen and twenty-five ministers; the federal cabinet is often substantially larger, while the territorial cabinets (six to eight) and that of Prince Edward Island (nine to twelve) are smaller.

Canadian cabinets are single-party creatures. Coalition governments, in which two or more political parties hold cabinet posts, are all but unknown. By contrast, coalition cabinets are commonplace in European multiparty democracies and are frequently found in Anglo-Celtic Westminster systems such as Ireland, Australia, and New Zealand.

Canadian cabinets are drawn almost exclusively from the ranks of elected legislators. Indeed, a defining feature of British-style responsible government is that ministers must be members of the elected parliament or legislature (in contrast to such polities as the United States and France, where ministers are not permitted to hold legislative office). Deviations from this custom are rare and temporary, though they are less exceptional in Canada than in other Westminster countries.

Within Canadian cabinets, first ministers dominate. The securing of power through electoral victory often rests primarily with the party leader, putting him or her in an inherently powerful position. And long-established convention accords the first minister unquestioned authority to choose the ministers, the portfolios they hold, and whether they remain in cabinet. Although this prerogative is hemmed in by numerous political constraints, as is the first minister's capacity to impose decisions on cabinet, the raw power of the first minister is formidable. Indeed, the first order of business in this audit is an examination, in the next chapter, of the charge that Canadian prime ministers and premiers are little better than elected dictators.

Canadian cabinets are highly institutionalized and extensively bureaucratized. Cabinet meetings unfold according to precise routine, and detailed procedures govern the submission of documents to cabinet. Large, influential government offices, known as central agencies, exist largely or solely to provide administrative and policy support to cabinet and to control cabinet processes. All but the smallest cabinets employ subcommittees, with some cabinets characterized by extensive networks of committees. Ministers also have call – both as individuals and collectively – on partisan staff and advisors, sometimes in great numbers.

Canadian cabinet ministers are, as a group, impermanent and homogeneous. Ministers typically come to office with little or no legislative experience, have relatively short-lived ministerial careers, and change portfolio assignments within cabinet frequently. In terms of social composition, Canada's cabinet ministers are remarkably homogeneous: overwhelmingly able-bodied, middle-aged, middle-class males of European heritage. This is unsurprising, given that they are drawn from legislatures numerically dominated by able-bodied, middle-aged, middle-class males of European heritage. At the same time, first ministers are at some pain to ensure that their cabinets are as inclusive as possible of all regions and of certain politically salient social groupings: the so-called representational imperative of Canadian cabinet making.

Historical Developments

The story of how over several centuries the modern cabinet emerged in Britain from the king's circle of personal advisors (the privy council) is an important and fascinating one, but need not be retold here (Jennings 1965; Mackintosh 1962). By the time of Confederation in 1867, all of the central constitutional and political principles that structure cabinet government in Canada to this day were already in place. Nevertheless, important changes in cabinet structure, composition, and operation have occurred, mostly within the past few decades.

In reviewing these changes we should bear in mind two key features of Canadian cabinet government. First is the paradox that the central law-making body in the land is itself all but invisible in the statute books. "There is," writes one close student of Canadian cabinets, "no law or document that specifically defines the cabinet or its responsibilities" (Matheson 1976, 1). Federally, provincially, and territorially, statutes set out certain limited features of cabinets – ministers' salaries, conflict of interest provisions and the like – but say little if anything about cabinet structure, composition, process, or powers. Some cabinet committees such as Treasury Board enjoy formal legal status, but the practical significance of this is minimal. The Constitution Act, 1982 establishes a Queen's Privy Council for Canada, and the commonly found term "governor in council" is legalese for cabinet, and yet this is as misleading as it is helpful. The Privy Council, which almost never meets, is composed of all former ministers (who, by virtue of their membership in this august body, are entitled to be called "honourable" for life), plus a few other assorted worthies and notables. In short, the federal cabinet is a committee (and a smallish one at that) of the Privy Council with no explicit status in the written Constitution. The only reference in the Constitution Act to the prime minister is an obscure, and now exhausted, provision requiring the prime minister to convene conferences on the constitutional status of Aboriginal peoples during the 1980s. Almost the only other legal reference to the prime minister is a 1935 order in council (cabinet decision) setting out in formal and not very enlightening terms certain of the prime minister's powers (Hunt 1995, 425-6). As Patrick Weller puts it in the Australian context: "cabinet is a committee of politicians unrecognised by the constitution, but attributed by convention with the final authority of government" (Weller 1992b, 5). Provinces and territories have no equivalent to the Privy Council, and while each typically has an act establishing an executive council (i.e., cabinet), these provide almost no insight into the real powers and workings of their cabinets.

The second key feature is a critical consequence of the first. The lack of formal legal definition of cabinet structure and operation permits enormous flexibility. This by no means implies that cabinets or prime ministers are entirely unfettered in their powers. The provisions of responsible government, outlined in the previous chapter, at once empower and constrain cabinet. So too the limits placed on government by the Charter and other pre-Charter principles reflecting the fundamental authority of the rule of law restrict cabinet's powers. Rather, as will become evident in the following discussion, cabinet enjoys tremendous flexibility in terms of its organization (size, formal structure, and so on), its processes, and its composition.

Perhaps the most evident change over the years has been in the size of cabinet. John A. Macdonald's first cabinet in 1867 comprised a baker's dozen ministers, while provincially, Ontario had but five and Nova Scotia four (first ministers included). As the scale and complexity of government expanded, at first gradually then almost exponentially, the number of ministers deemed necessary to run it likewise grew. If on occasion cabinets experienced short-lived minor reductions in size, the long-term trend was continuous growth. In 1907 the average provincial cabinet contained 6.7 ministers, while the federal cabinet stood at 15. Provincial cabinets grew to an average of nearly 11 by the 1940s, to 17.5 in the early 1970s, and to 22.7 in the late 1980s (White 1998, 374). Nationally, the cabinet, 20 by 1947, grew to 30 in 1973 and reached 40 under Prime Minister Mulroney in the late 1980s. The 1990s obsession with restraint begat a significant reversal of the long-term trend: Prime Minister Chrétien's first cabinet in 1993 was pared to 23, while the average provincial cabinet fell to just under 19 (White 1998, 374). In the less straitened economic climate of the new millennium, the symbolism of smaller cabinets has been of lesser political moment: in early 2004, the federal cabinet consisted of 28 ministers, assisted by another 11 junior ministers (secretaries of state); provincially the average had grown marginally to 19.4.

Less obvious but almost certainly of greater consequence has been the thoroughgoing institutionalization of Canadian cabinets. In the nineteenth century, the prime minister answered much of his own correspondence personally, in longhand. As late as the 1960s and 1970s, ministers in some provinces held down close to full-time jobs outside cabinet. Some provincial cabinet meetings were conducted without benefit of written agendas or formal records of decisions, and only the most rudimentary systems existed for processing cabinet documents.

Ministers had always had departmental bureaucrats to advise and assist them, but until the 1960s they typically lacked personal staff beyond a secretary; as a collectivity, cabinet was likewise bereft of professional support. Most Canadian governments have long had a treasury board, a committee of ministers charged with overseeing financial outlays, but other cabinet committees appeared only in the recent past.

Cabinet institutionalization came to Canada in the 1940s, but took hold only slowly. In Ottawa, the press of business arising from the war effort convinced Prime Minister King to follow the British lead and develop a small cabinet secretariat (Heeney 1967). More innovative and influential was the creation just a few years later by the Saskatchewan CCF of powerful, professional political-bureaucratic agencies – "central agencies" in modern parlance – to support the ideologically driven planning of cabinet and its newly established committees (Dunn 1995). Similar developments were slow to take root elsewhere in Canada; even in Ontario, with its large, complex government, cabinet committees were of little consequence and central agencies carried little weight until the massive reforms of the early 1970s (Schindeler 1969; Stewart 1989).

The 1970s, however, were marked by extensive cabinet institutionalization across Canada: powerful central agencies, extensive committee systems, highly formalized procedures for cabinet documentation and decision making, and substantial entourages of personal ministerial staff became the order of the day. Most jurisdictions established a layer of parliamentary secretaries or assistants, government members elevated somewhat above the normal run of backbenchers to assist ministers. Ebbs and flows have been evident in the extent and significance of various elements of the "institutionalized cabinet," but its hallmark features persist: "shared knowledge [among ministers], collegial decision making and formulation of government-wide priorities and objectives" (Dupré 1985, 235). Nowhere has there been anything like a return to the "unaided" cabinets of the 1950s and 1960s (Dunn 1995).

The most noteworthy other changes relate to the social composition of cabinet and to the career patterns of ministers. Reflecting broader societal changes, women – largely or wholly excluded from cabinets until the 1970s – have since come to hold ministerial office in increasing numbers, as have nonwhite Canadians. For the most part, however, these changes have been slow and limited in scope: only in rare instances has the proportion of women in Canadian cabinets approached 50 percent. For example, in Ontario NDP premier Bob Rae's first cabinet in 1990, eleven of twenty-three ministers were women, and in the Liberal Yukon cabinet in 2002, four of eight ministers, including Premier Pat Duncan, were women. Canada-wide, a recent tally shows that 23 percent of ministers were women (Trimble and Arscott 2003, 148). Given that women form a slight majority in the general population, this figure underlines the distance women still have to travel to reach numerical equality around the cabinet table. As for the best seat at the table, women's underrepresentation is even more pronounced: only five women have ever served as first minister. Three of the five headed small jurisdictions – Nellie Cournyea in the Northwest Territories, Pat Duncan in the Yukon, and Catherine Callbeck in Prince Edward Island – while the other two – Kim Campbell in Ottawa and Rita Johnston in British Columbia – held office for only a few months.

Definitive numbers are not available for visible minorities, but they too are clearly underrepresented in comparison to their share of the population. The appointment of a minister from a visible minority community is still sufficiently unusual as to render it newsworthy. And, as with women, it is even rarer yet for a person of non-European descent to hold the top job, though India-born Ujjal Dosanjh served as BC premier and Joe Ghiz, who was of Lebanese heritage, was premier of PEI. The notable exception to this rule is that since 1991, every premier of Nunavut and the Northwest Territories has been Aboriginal.

A substantial but not often noticed shift has occurred in the age profile of Canadian ministers. While modern-day Canadian cabinets have only marginally higher proportions of ministers under forty, older ministers are far less in evidence than just a few decades ago: in the 1940s and 1950s, nearly half of provincial ministers remained in cabinet past their sixtieth birthday and 14 percent were still in office into their seventies. By the 1990s, only 11 percent of ministers were still in office in their sixties and a barely perceptible 0.3 percent lasted into their seventies (White 1998, 378-9).

Even more dramatic have been changes in the contours of the political careers of Canadian cabinet ministers. The pattern in the 1940s and 1950s was for ministers to stay in cabinet for substantial periods (the provincial mean was just under 10 years) and to enjoy extended tenure in their portfolios (mean: 5.2 years). By the 1990s, ministerial careers had become far more ephemeral: the average provincial minister served in cabinet for only 3.9 years and could expect to stay in a given portfolio for just twenty-four months. The implications for the interpersonal dynamics of cabinets and for the nature of cabinet decision making are substantial (White 1998).

Ministers' careers have become shorter and their time in individual portfolios has declined because cabinet shuffles have become so frequent. First ministers shuffle their cabinets for a variety of reasons: to reward solid performers and remove political deadwood; to give the appearance of freshness and progress; to respond to ministerial departures, voluntary and otherwise; to complement structural reorganizations; and to alter the political composition or outlook of cabinet. Comparative data are hard to come by, but Canadian first ministers appear to shuffle their cabinets more often than their counterparts in other Westminster systems. Frequent and extensive shuffles are a defining feature of the modern-day Canadian cabinet.

Cabinet Composition

Canadians have a good deal of experience with minority governments, in which a single-party cabinet governs without a clear legislative majority. Save during the chaotic and unstable pre-Confederation era in the United Province of Canada, however, coalition (multiparty) governments have never been common, and today they have all but disappeared from the scene. Nationally, the only episode of coalition government occurred during the Great War. Provincially, coalition governments enjoyed more currency, most notably in Manitoba from 1928 to 1958 and in British Columbia in the 1940s and early 1950s. Since then, the only Canadian experience of coalition government has been in Yukon in the 1990s and in Saskatchewan for two years following the 1999 election. These are highly atypical aberrations: Canadian cabinets are very much one-party governments (though political parties can often be understood as coalitions or alliances of internal factions).

While the vast majority of ministers are drawn from the ranks of elected parliamentarians, this is not a hard and fast rule. No written requirement dictates that ministers hold elected office or, in Ottawa, be members of the Senate. John Turner was not the first to serve as prime minister of Canada without a seat in either the Commons or the Senate. Federally and provincially, the lists of nonmembers appointed to cabinet are substantial (Parliament of Canada 2003). Nor is this practice some long-eclipsed historical oddity. Prime Minister Chrétien appointed three non-MPs to cabinet: Stéphane Dion and Pierre Pettigrew in 1996 and Brian Tobin in 2000. (Tobin had been an MP, but at the time of his appointment was premier of Newfoundland.) A powerful constitutional convention, however, ensures that once appointed to cabinet, ministers must in short order win elected office. All three sought and won election soon after being appointed to cabinet.

The selection of these three Liberal ministers reflected the prime minister's assessment of their personal abilities and political strengths, but such appointments may serve other purposes. First ministers who wish to widen the representational ambit of their cabinets occasionally do so by bringing nonlegislators into the fold: BC premier Ujjal Dosanjh appointed prominent Aboriginal leader Ed John to his cabinet in 2001; in Nova Scotia, Premier Donald Cameron brought two women into his cabinet in 1993, there being none in his caucus.

While it is permissible to serve in cabinet without holding elected office, however, it is not permissible to do so for long. Ministers appointed in this fashion must soon secure a seat, either through a general election or through a by-election in what the party trusts is a "safe" seat. The force and import of this convention is illustrated by the short-lived ministerial career of Pierre Juneau. Appointed to cabinet in August 1975 by Prime Minister Trudeau, two months later Juneau lost a by-election in a supposedly safe Liberal seat, whereupon he immediately resigned from cabinet. Given the firm, if unwritten, requirement that unelected ministers quickly become elected ministers, the practice of occasionally appointing nonparliamentarians to cabinet hardly constitutes a serious affront to democratic precepts.

Judgments about senators who hold cabinet posts are not so clear-cut. (This is of course an issue only in Ottawa, for none of the provincial or territorial legislatures still have upper houses.) Even in the nineteenth century, it was uncommon for more than two or three senators to hold ministerial office at one time (it is probably coincidental that the only senator to serve as prime minister, Mackenzie Bowell, regularly ranks at or near the top of worst prime minister lists). In recent times, all federal cabinets have had at least one senator, who serves as leader of the government in the Senate but usually has limited or no departmental responsibilities. Occasionally, however, prime ministers attempt to meet the obligations of the representational imperative – especially its regional dimension – by appointing senators to significant portfolio assignments. Prime Minister Trudeau, whose Liberal Party was all but bereft of Western MPs following the 1980 election, and Prime Minister Clark, whose Progressive Conservative government (1979-80) was severely lacking in MPs from Quebec, both employed this gambit.

The practice of appointing nonparliamentarians to ministerial office comes close to being a uniquely Canadian phenomenon. While not unknown in Britain, decades pass between occurrences; the last such appointment was in the early 1960s. In New Zealand and Ireland formal constitutional provisions explicitly prohibit unelected ministers.

A related practice, common in Canada but unusual in other Anglo-Celtic Westminster systems, is the wholesale appointment of ministers immediately upon their first election. Staggering proportions of Canadian ministers take up their duties having had little or no legislative experience. From the 1940s to the 1990s, between a quarter and a third of all provincial ministers came to office without having ever sat either in opposition or on the government backbenches. Fully 75 percent of all provincial ministers in this period spent nary a single day in opposition prior to their appointment to cabinet (White 1998, 375-7). By contrast, at Westminster over roughly the same period the average minister had spent 12.2 years in the Commons before being appointed to cabinet, and fewer than 10 percent of ministers arrived at cabinet within five years of their first election (de Winter 1991, 48). Even in New Zealand, where the small numbers of members might be expected to induce appointment of neophyte ministers, a strong norm exists that would-be ministers must serve at least three years on the backbench (McLeay 1995, 47). The widespread lack of parliamentary experience among Canadian ministers can hardly fail to colour their attitudes toward the opposition, government backbenchers, and indeed the entire legislative process. It is unhealthy for Canadian democracy for so many ministers to attain office without experiencing life as a private member.

The Representational Imperative

Political science students — and Canadians generally — are often shocked to learn that first ministers may decide whom to include in cabinet on the basis of social characteristics rather than on merit. Certainly the very best and brightest, as well as the most senior figures in the caucus, are appointed to cabinet with little consideration of social characteristics. Beyond this initial core, however, first ministers are constrained in their cabinet choices by what has been termed the "representational imperative" (Campbell 1985). Simply put, it has become a deeply ingrained tenet of Canadian politics that, so far as possible, all regions and all politically salient groups should have representatives in cabinet. In consequence, "every cabinet must contain at least a few dullards or nonentities to represent some important interest" (Matheson 1976, 29).

Ideas of what constitutes "politically salient" do of course change over time. In the nineteenth century and well into the twentieth, religious affiliation was a prominent social characteristic, putting first ministers at pains to ensure adequate representation of Catholics and Protestants (and indeed within Protestantism, Anglicans, Methodists, Presbyterians, and so on). For much of this period as well, ethnicity was important, defined in terms of English, French, Irish, and Scots. By contrast, the notion of appointing women to cabinet was simply beyond the pale. In twenty-first-century Canada, religion has lost much of its political salience – few know or care about the religious affiliations of political leaders – while ethnicity still looms large, though the categories have changed to visible minorities, "white" Europeans, and so on. And no first minister would even contemplate an all-male cabinet.

If social groups' political significance has waxed and waned over time, one social factor remains critical in cabinet representation: region. Every province (save sometimes Prince Edward Island) *must* be represented in the federal cabinet, and in suitable numbers. Some provinces may have to be satisfied with a single minister, but Ontario and Quebec each requires a sizable ministerial contingent. The largest cities – Vancouver, Toronto, and Montreal – must have several ministers; significant regions in larger provinces, such as northern Ontario, must also be accommodated if at all possible. Provincially, regionalism is no less compelling in cabinet composition, though as discussed below the delineation of regions may not be so clear-cut as at the national level.

Discussion of the democratic outcomes of the representational imperative are reserved for Chapter 5, but it is worth noting at this juncture that this practice reflects more than simply crass politics through efforts to curry favour with politically powerful interests, though political gain is hardly irrelevant. When John A. Macdonald crafted the first national cabinet he did so with an eye to using it as a device for unifying – substantively as well as symbolically – the disparate regions and cultural groupings that had been uneasily grafted together in Confederation. He therefore followed the principles of cabinet representation that had emerged in the pre-Confederation Province of Canada, and in turn his successors institutionalized his approach into a powerful political convention.

In consequence, the Canadian cabinet is a good deal larger than it might otherwise be, the position of the prime minister is enhanced, and the overall competence of cabinet suffers to some degree (not only are the mediocre elevated to cabinet, but the truly able may be excluded because cabinet already contains enough ministers who share their social characteristics). The nature of cabinet decision making is also affected, as are channels and dimensions of ministerial influence. This is most evident in the phenomenon of regional ministers, who exercise extensive political and administrative clout in their provinces or regions, quite independent of their portfolio responsibilities (Bakvis 1991). Though not unknown in provincial governments, the regional minister system has primarily been in evidence around the cabinet table in Ottawa. Finally, the Canadian proclivity for bringing into cabinet those without elected office owes a good deal to the representational imperative.

At the national level, the representational imperative is tied to an important cabinet function: "cabinet has reflected both the federal and pluralistic nature of Canadian society and has played an important role in counteracting the immobilizing and unstabilizing effects of Canadian pluralism" (Matheson 1976, 22). But provincial societies are far more homogeneous; few experience the strong centripetal regional and cultural pressures that pervade national politics and arguably necessitate a broadly representative national cabinet. Why, then, does the representational imperative seem as strong in provincial (and indeed in territorial) politics as it is nationally? The most straightforward explanation holds that Canadians have simply come to believe that this is how cabinets ought to be constructed and how they ought to operate. It need not be this way: in no other Anglo-Celtic Westminster system does representation of regions and social groupings have anything like the political compulsion it does in Canada.

Structure and Process

Canadian cabinets typically comprise a relatively large number of small departments. British and Australian cabinets, in contrast, are characterized by departments fewer in number but substantially wider in scope (Aucoin and Bakvis 1993). This difference is in turn related to a typical, though not universal, feature of cabinets in this country: their single-tier structure. In Canada the term "cabinet minister" is, in most cases, redundant: save in the few instances noted below, all ministers sit in cabinet. Not so elsewhere. In Britain, for example, barely more than twenty "secretaries of state" are cabinet ministers; a second tier, called "ministers of state," do not usually attend cabinet though they may exercise significant jurisdictional responsibility subject to the direction of their secretary of state. Below them is another tier of yet more junior ministers, styled "parliamentary undersecretaries," with substantially less political and administrative clout. Hence the British ministry may number over a hundred ministers, only a few of whom are cabinet ministers. Though not so large or complex, the Australian ministry also includes cabinet and noncabinet ministers.

Although Canadian federal ministers "not of cabinet" can be found as early as 1869, the practice ended in the 1920s and, given their small numbers — usually one or two, never more than four — they hardly constituted a clear principle of organizational design. Though not formally described as such, Prime Minister Clark's short-lived government (1979-80) was structured into inner and outer cabinets (Weller 1980). When Prime Minister Chrétien took office in 1993, he instituted a formally tiered cabinet with twenty-three full cabinet ministers and eight junior, noncabinet ministers. Prime Minister Martin abandoned the two-tier structure when he took office in 2004. Following a major cabinet shuffle and government reorganization in 1993, Bob Rae's government in Ontario also adopted a two-tiered model, with twenty cabinet ministers and another seven junior ministers who did not attend cabinet, but the experiment ended with the election of the Harris Progressive Conservatives two years later.

Whereas the rationale for two- or three-tiered cabinets in the United Kingdom and Australia is primarily organizational effectiveness, in Canada this motive is probably secondary to the relentless pressure of the representational imperative: in Ottawa the ministers of state (i.e., junior ministers, formerly called "secretaries of state") are more likely to be drawn from the ranks of identifiable and underrepresented groups – Aboriginal people, women, visible minorities – than are full-fledged cabinet ministers.

To highlight the general absence of tiered cabinets in Canada is not to suggest that all ministers are equal. Far from it. Both formal and informal ministerial pecking orders are evident, if constantly shifting. A few ministers, most often in the larger or more politically sensitive departments (health, for example) in the larger jurisdictions, are explicitly designated as associate or assistant ministers subject to the direction of the lead departmental minister. Though clearly of secondary status, they nonetheless attend cabinet meetings. In all cabinets, at all times, however, certain ministers wield extensive power by virtue of their portfolios, personal strengths, standing in the party, or personal links to the first minister. After the prime minister or premier, finance ministers are normally the most powerful; those holding high-spending or strategically important portfolios (health, education, or economic development) typically carry greater clout than colleagues in small, less significant portfolios (tourism, citizenship, or culture). In short, the distribution of power within cabinet is markedly unequal.

Among the minor dramatis personae of Canadian cabinet government are parliamentary secretaries and parliamentary assistants (called "legislative assistants" in Manitoba). These are elected members of the government party assigned by the first minister to assist ministers. They are not junior ministers and their influence is generally limited; they are more akin to run-of-the-mill backbenchers than to ministers. Their duties are largely contingent on their ministers' willingness to share power and are highly variable, ranging from standing in for the minister to cut ribbons and speechify to taking administrative and political responsibility for significant policy sectors. A parliamentary assistantship can sometimes serve as a testing or training ground for a would-be minister, but such a position is certainly no guarantee of a subsequent cabinet appointment (Glenn 1997). Prime Minister Martin elevated the status of parliamentary secretaries, appointing them to the Privy Council and, more important, entrusting some with important policy initiatives, which entails their attendance at cabinet meetings for specific agenda items.

Beyond size and the presence or absence of formal tiers of ministers, the principal structural questions about cabinets relate to their committees. Little point would be served in enumerating the dizzying array of cabinet committees to be found across Canada (for details see Dunn 1995 and Dunn 2002) but some general observations are in order. All Canadian cabinets, save in Nunavut and Yukon, have committees, many of which exercise substantial power. Not surprisingly, the larger cabinets tend to have the most extensive committee systems, in order to make the best use of that terribly scarce resource, ministerial time, especially when cabinet numbers twenty or more. The decision-making style of the first minister (who ultimately decides on the number, scope, and influence of cabinet committees) and the political priorities of the day also affect cabinet committee systems. For example, governments focused primarily on program reductions and spending cuts, such as the first Chrétien administration and the Harris cabinet in Ontario, may prefer a streamlined cabinet organization to facilitate quick, sweeping change and thus sharply reduce the number and influence of cabinet committees. By contrast, governments concerned with expanding the scope of government and developing new policy ventures are generally more inclined to employ cabinet committees, which are especially useful when interdepartmental coordination or extensive ministerial discussion are thought necessary. For the most part, the composition of cabinet committees parallels, in unremarkable fashion, that of full cabinet, but some potentially important variations exist. In tiered cabinets, noncabinet ministers typically attend cabinet committees on a regular basis. More interestingly, in some cabinets, backbench government members attend cabinet committee meetings on a sporadic or even routine basis. Chapter 4 explores this practice.

The routing of cabinet business – for example whether an issue is referred to cabinet committee before or after full cabinet considers it, or whether the policy and financial implications of a pending decision are considered separately, sequentially, or simultaneously – varies a good deal. So too some cabinet committees constitute the real site of decision making, with full cabinet essentially rubber-stamping committee decisions, but in other instances cabinet committees play an advisory role only. Most Canadian cabinets have central planning and priorities committees, but their actual functions and influence vary widely. Such apparently mundane organizational concerns may have important democratic consequences. These are addressed in Chapter 5.

The frequency of cabinet meetings carries no great pertinence for democratic governance but is worth noting. Typically, full cabinet meets once a week most of the year (less often in high summer) and every year stages one or two retreats of two or three days. Variations from this norm are common; in some provinces, for example, cabinet meets at least briefly every day the House is sitting. Most cabinet committees meet every two or three weeks, though here the variations are greater; some committees don't meet for months on end and others may meet several times a week, at least for short periods.

Cabinets are highly secretive. Again, this is very much the norm for executive bodies in all systems of governance. Even though all Canadian jurisdictions have comprehensive freedom-of-information (FOI) legislation, cabinet documents remain closely guarded secrets, typically exempt from FOI incursions. To be sure, leaks of cabinet confidences are commonplace in modern-day politics (the ship of state, as one wag has it, is the only one that leaks from the top), but legal methods of obtaining cabinet documents – submissions, records of discussion, and decisions – are extremely limited, save in the very long (two or three decades) term. The possibilities and their democratic implications are explored in Chapter 4.

Staff Support

Canadian cabinets collectively and ministers individually have call on the enormous bureaucratic resources of government. In more concrete terms (and in keeping with the core executive concept), cabinet staff support is realized through three quite diverse sets of officials: deputy ministers, central agencies, and personal political staff. The democratic implications of these support systems are examined in Chapter 5.

Ministers with charge of government departments tend to rely heavily on their deputy ministers. A deputy minister is not, despite the misleading title, an elected official of ministerial rank, but rather the appointed bureaucrat holding the highest administrative position in a government department. Most deputies are career bureaucrats with long and varied service in a range of public service positions. As a rule they are tremendously capable and possessed of finely honed, "small-p" political skills. In most jurisdictions few deputies have backgrounds in party politics, though in some jurisdictions deputies with partisan ties are not unusual. Though nonpartisan and politically neutral, deputies nonetheless work very closely with ministers. Increasingly, their strong suit is managerial and leadership ability, rather than specialized policy expertise, and accordingly deputies find themselves shuffled to new departments almost as often as ministers are. As the bureaucratic heads of government departments they channel the expertise, support, and advice of the entire administrative apparatus of the department – often several thousand civil servants – to the minister. Significantly, while deputies work in close concert with their ministers and report directly to them, they owe their appointment to the first minister. In some jurisdictions this entails a clear responsibility and reporting relationship to him or her, though in Ottawa and some provinces a more arms-length relationship is the norm.

Central agencies are relatively small government departments whose prime mission is to support and advise the first minister and key individual ministers, as well as cabinet as a whole and its committees. Their direct dealings with the public or organized interests are very limited. Most central agencies are administrative, in that they are headed and staffed by permanent civil servants. The most important of these nonpolitical central agencies is usually the cabinet or executive council office (the Privy Council Office in Ottawa). Others include finance departments, public service commissions, and treasury or management board secretariats; some governments have intergovernmental affairs secretariats or additional specialized agencies. In addition, each government has one exceptionally powerful political central agency – the Premier's or Prime Minister's Office – staffed by highly partisan political operatives intensely loyal to the first minister (though some purely administrative positions may be filled by nonpartisan civil servants). By virtue of their close and direct links to the first minister, the key figures in this office may wield exceptional power and accordingly elicit strong criticism from political friend and foe alike. Over the years what once typically amounted to a fusion of the first minister's office and the cabinet office has largely given way to a clear division of labour – with a close working relationship – between the bureaucratic and the political central agencies, though in some provinces, such as Nova Scotia, the demarcation remains blurry.

The department of finance (or equivalent) is the central repository of the government's economic expertise and plays a crucial role in setting overall economic policy as well as in individual spending decisions. Its mandate is to advise and support the finance minister, who is, after the first minister, normally the most powerful minister in cabinet owing to the pivotal role of financial considerations in government decision making – and also owing to the advantage of having the expertise and clout of the finance department at his or her disposal. The treasury board secretariat or equivalent also has significant influence over spending decisions (and may deal with other management issues such as labour relations), but usually has less influence than the finance department. The treasury board secretariat may exist as a standalone entity with its own minister or as a wing of the finance department. In Ottawa and in other jurisdictions, the treasury board secretariat provides analysis and advice to the cabinet committee (the Treasury Board) charged with reviewing individual expenditure decisions.

Other cabinet committees are staffed and supported by officials in the cabinet office. This may involve a certain degree of policy expertise – offering alternative sources of information and advice to that put forward by the operating departments – but the cabinet office's more significant function, indeed the source of its often substantial influence, is managing the cabinet decision-making process and the flow of cabinet documents. This may sound decidedly mundane and inconsequential; it is anything but. Control of the cabinet agenda and oversight of the decision-making process – with the first minister's sanction – carry the potential for significant power and influence.

Personal political staff (sometimes called "exempt staff" because they are exempt from normal civil service rules on hiring and political activity) are each minister's equivalent of the first minister's office. All cabinet ministers have at least a few staff in their office, paid out of public funds, who perform explicitly partisan political tasks. They tend to be confirmed party faithful (and often quite young, because of the job's horrendous demands on time and energy) with strong personal commitment to the minister: if their minister is shuffled to another portfolio, they will usually also move to the new department, in contrast to the nonpartisan bureaucrats, who remain in their posts when ministers change. When ministers lose their jobs through resignation or dismissal, or when the government changes, the personal staff are likewise rendered jobless. (A controversial exception occurs in Ottawa, where exempt staff with three years' service are entitled to positions of equivalent status in the public service. What might be seen as the politicization of the bureaucracy occasions substantial heartburn among those who prize a politically neutral public service.)

Ministers' political staff write speeches; proffer policy and political advice; maintain political links with the first minister's office, government backbenchers, party members, interest groups, and others; and serve as liaison with the permanent officials. This liaison function covers a multitude of possibilities. Much is routine communication and coordination; for example, the public servants might provide the raw information for a minister's Question Period preparation, whereas the political staff would put the political spin on it. The relationship is not always cooperative and benign, however. Some ministers and some governments, distrustful of the permanent bureaucracy, look to political staff as a counterweight to the bureaucrats' influence or as a means of imposing political control over them. For their part, the bureaucrats sometimes view the political staff as meddlesome hacks attempting to exert improper influence in what should be politically neutral processes. This can and does lead to antagonism and conflict, but cooperative and mutually respectful dynamics generally characterize the interplay of political staff and public servants.

As noted above, ministers having personal political staff is a fairly recent phenomenon. Once established, though, the idea took hold far more quickly and extensively in Canada than in other Anglo-Celtic Westminster systems. This may reflect proximity to the United States, where members of Congress employ legions of staff. But Canada is now less distinct on this dimension than in the past. Indeed, one assessment suggests that, at least under the Hawke Labor government (1983-91), Australian ministers "tended to rely upon their personal staffs much more than would their Canadian or British opposite numbers" (Campbell and Halligan 1992, 7-8). Canadian ministers are still substantially less likely than their counterparts in other Anglo-Celtic Westminster systems to follow the British tradition of seconding permanent public servants to work as ministers' personal staff. Federal ministers typically employ a dozen to a score political staff; in one extraordinary case, the minister's office swelled to over a hundred (though many of these were seconded civil servants; Bakvis 1991, 191). In the largest provinces, ministers burdened with large or politically sensitive portfolios commonly employ a dozen or more political staff, though half that number is more usual. In the smaller provinces, most ministers make do with no more than four political staff (these numbers exclude purely clerical or secretarial staff).

The Cabinet at Work

The foregoing discussion of the characteristics, composition, and structure of Canadian cabinets and core executives provides essential background for our audit, but it is also useful to gain a flesh-and-blood appreciation of the cabinet at work. Accordingly, this section attempts to give a sense of what transpires in a cabinet or cabinet committee meeting. It is a composite picture, drawn from cabinets across the country; doubtless every Canadian cabinet differs at least slightly, if not substantially, from this account.

Cabinet meetings take up only a small proportion of ministers' time. The typical ministers' day – again, a composite, for no typical minister or typical ministerial day exists – is long and onerous. Often beginning with a breakfast meeting for a staff briefing or consultations with interest group leaders, it frequently doesn't end until late in the evening following a dinner speech to a political organization or trade association (perhaps a long drive or flight from the capital), a late-night sitting of the House, or some other official event. In between, staff squeeze in endless meetings and telephone calls to deal with ongoing policy issues, emerging crises, political strategizing, constituency business, and the like. If the House is in session, the minister will attend at least part of the day's proceedings. This requires careful briefing on issues that may arise during Question Period. As well, ministers are constantly travelling, both on government business and, for ministers whose ridings are not in or near the capital, to attend constituency functions and spend time at home with family. Somewhere during this hectic schedule the minister must find time to sign letters and official documents; read, or at least skim, the numberless documents with which he is expected to be familiar; and – perhaps most important – reflect on what he wants to accomplish and how to do so.

Two or three days before cabinet meets, each minister receives a large binder, compiled by cabinet office staff, with background material on the issues to be discussed at the meeting. For issues requiring discussion and decision, the cabinet submission from the sponsoring department contains an executive summary of perhaps two or three pages setting out the problem, possible solutions, and the proposed course of action; extensive appendices provide detailed information. Unless a minister's department stands to be directly and substantially affected by another minister's proposal, she will read only the executive summary. In fact, ministers don't usually find the time to read all the executive summaries before the meeting. The minister's officials alert her to issues or submissions bearing on her portfolio and suggest what lines the departmental response should follow.

The cabinet room is dominated by a large oval table, with one or two small side tables for officials taking notes and a few chairs around the perimeter of the room. The first minister generally sits at the middle of one side, though some prefer the end of the table. Those ministers seated closest to him are the most powerful, by virtue of experience, portfolio, or personal ties. Newly appointed or junior ministers are relegated to the ends of the table. Places at the table are restricted to ministers; even the most senior officials, such as the cabinet secretary, sit behind the ministers, though some first ministers prefer having the cabinet secretary beside them at the table. Nonministers rarely speak during cabinet meetings, and then only when asked for their views or for information. When they wish to add something to the discussion, they pass notes to the first minister or to other members of cabinet.

Access to the cabinet room is a closely guarded privilege. No more than a handful of nonministers are routinely in the room: two or three senior cabinet office officials and one or two of the first minister's top political staff, perhaps the chief of staff and the head of communications. Other top bureaucrats and politicos may be present for discussion of specific items but will be asked to leave once the item is completed. Ministers' political staff do not attend cabinet. Cabinet rooms usually have antechambers where officials wait to be called into the meeting and ministers make phone calls or consult with their staff about upcoming agenda items.

The format of cabinet agendas varies a good deal, but meetings follow an established routine, typically beginning with standard reports, such as the House leader's report on parliamentary business or lists of proposed appointees to important government jobs. These reports are primarily for information purposes and are not normally subject to debate. Reports from cabinet committees may generate extensive debate but more often are simply approved on the nod. The heart of the meeting is usually discussion of new policy initiatives – proposals contained in formal submissions coming forward from specific ministers. Central agencies enforce rules about timely and proper preparation of these submissions, in order to ensure that ministers' time is not wasted dealing with imprecise or incomplete submissions. Ministers, however, do not always comply with the rules and sometimes attempt to finesse the system with a "walk-in," literally walking into cabinet with a request that no one knew about beforehand. Ministers do not appreciate colleagues asking for approval of projects with no advance warning or background information, which makes walk-ins risky, but every cabinet experiences them. Some jurisdictions have a standing agenda item allowing ministers to briefly raise matters of concern without notice or supporting paperwork; this practice reduces but does not eliminate walk-ins.

Cabinet debates are far shorter and better focused than parliamentary debates. With ministerial time such a precious commodity, long, rambling speeches are not tolerated; ministers' comments are expected to be brief and to the point. Usually just a few interested and involved ministers take part in discussions on routine items; those who have nothing to contribute to the debate are expected to stay silent. On major, controversial, or divisive issues, all ministers may weigh in, with discussion extending over several meetings, but such issues are exceptional. The first minister sets the tenor of debate: some will not abide strong language and raised voices, while others encourage ministers to speak their minds and accept the occasional screaming match as the price of vigorous debate. By and large, though, ministers' comments in debate are measured and temperate, though tough-minded and often critical or skeptical about their colleagues' proposals and requests.

Though the first minister may delegate the actual chairing of cabinet meetings to another minister, he is the one with the capacity to cut debate short and "call the consensus," specifying what cabinet has decided. Some first ministers occasionally ask for a show of hands on especially contentious or important issues, but for the most part formal votes in cabinet are rare; as discussed in Chapter 3, the first minister can "outvote" the entire cabinet. Officials take detailed notes, though not verbatim transcriptions of discussions. These notes are used to formulate official cabinet minutes and records of decision, over which the first minister has final say. Minutes are circulated to ministers and senior bureaucrats.

Cabinet committees vary more widely than full cabinets in size, composition, operating style, informal norms, and so on. Like full cabinet, their proceedings are based on extensive documentation circulated in advance of the meeting. With their narrower mandates and smaller size, however, they generally feature longer, more detailed discussion of policy or spending proposals. Attendance at cabinet committee is not so tightly restricted as at full cabinet; substantial numbers of bureaucratic officials and political advisors may be present for committee meetings. Nonministers may sit at the meeting table, rather than in the back of the room, and in some jurisdictions they participate freely in discussions.

Federal-Provincial Comparisons

Premised on identical constitutional precepts of responsible government – with all the implications for structure, operations, and power relationship that entails – and located within a broadly similar set of political traditions and values, provincial cabinets are in essentials closely akin to those in Ottawa. So are Yukon cabinets; the consensus government cabinets of Nunavut and the Northwest Territories differ significantly (see the next section). At the same time, systematic and substantial differences do exist between the two levels of government.

Scale and complexity are certainly factors, though on many dimensions – cabinet size and scope of committee systems, for example –

clear-cut federal-provincial contrasts are less in evidence than ranges of possibilities in which Ottawa is located at or near one pole. In at least one key area, however, these factors matter a good deal: the power of the first minister.

Although the formal powers of Canadian first ministers vary little, "provincial government is premier's government ... the extent of his authority is significantly greater than that of his federal counterpart" (Young and Morley 1983, 54). This is an observation about politics, rather than about constitutional position. Premiers have the capacity to dominate both their cabinets and their entire governments to a far greater extent than does the prime minister. The scale and complexity of government in even the largest provinces, let alone the smaller ones, is qualitatively different from that in Ottawa. Accordingly, the premier's greater knowledge of people, events, and processes in his or her jurisdiction, the less burdensome calls on the premier's time, and the smaller number of advisors and assistants necessary to manage government and to deal with problems on the premier's behalf all contribute to the premier's more advantageous position.

Perhaps the best illustration is the frequency with which even modern-day premiers are able to hold major portfolios. Though the demands of office have in recent years sharply reduced the number of premiers who take on major portfolio responsibilities, especially in the larger provinces, this does still occur. By contrast, it has been decades since the prime minister has been able to reserve for him- or herself significant portfolio responsibilities, though at key junctures the prime minister takes charge of the federal-provincial-territorial relations or constitutional and national unity files. The portfolio of choice when premiers take on departmental responsibilities is finance – typically the second most powerful post in cabinet – which increases their capacity for domination through involvement in detailed policy and management issues.

As with the premier, so too with ministers: the smaller scale and less complex character of provincial government offer provincial ministers greater scope for exercising personal control and direction over their portfolios. This generalization must be tempered with a recognition of important countervailing forces, such as the larger personal political staff available to federal ministers. Ministers holding the largest and most difficult provincial portfolios, such as health, are likely to be busier and faced with more complex issues and processes than some federal ministers.

Differences in size and complexity mean that at the federal level, cabinet as a collective body (as opposed to its committees or other offshoots) has travelled a good deal further down the road to what one British commentator called "disintegration" (Seymour-Ure 1971, 196). Aucoin and Bakvis have written of the federal cabinet that "the use of an elaborate committee system has meant that over time the idea of cabinet as an executive body has been diminished, if not eliminated altogether ... by the 1990s, the cabinet no longer functioned as an executive body" (Aucoin and Bakvis 1993, 409-10). Far more than in Ottawa, provincial cabinets remain genuine decision-making bodies.

Both individually and collectively, provincial ministers and cabinets find themselves in qualitatively different positions vis-à-vis their legislatures than do their federal counterparts. Provincial cabinets typically dominate their legislatures far more completely than the federal cabinet dominates Parliament. This is a function of the relatively small caucuses (government as well as opposition) in provincial houses and of the level and nature of procedural opportunities and staff support available to private members, which, save in Quebec and Ontario, are markedly inferior to those in Ottawa.

At the same time, the far smaller absolute numbers at the provincial level make for a markedly shallower talent pool of prospective ministers. We need not assume that national politics attracts superior politicians; the inexorable logic of proportions alone works against provincial cabinets. Provincial cabinets are typically 50 to 75 percent the size of the federal cabinet, but the government caucus at the provincial level is often only 15 to 30 percent as large as its federal counterpart. Consequently provincial cabinets necessarily include a higher proportion of second- or third-rate ministers than the federal cabinet.

The representational imperative, which is more institutionalized and predictable in Ottawa, plays out rather differently provincially.

First, region is much more precisely defined at the national level; primarily it equates to province, though in the larger provinces, which are allocated several cabinet posts, urban-hinterland distinctions and sub-provincial regions must be considered. Although provincial premiers must carefully balance regional considerations in filling cabinet posts, regional lines are more fluid at the provincial level (where exactly does eastern Ontario begin?). The proportionately larger number of cabinet jobs to be spread over a smaller number of regions also gives premiers substantially more flexibility in meeting the regional imperative. For example, the notion of a region having "too many" ministers is a serious constraint at the national level, where it could be politically dodgy to have, say, three Newfoundland or two Winnipeg ministers. Rarely is this an issue provincially.

Second, though over the years the influence of regional political ministers in Ottawa has waxed and waned while the formal and informal channels through which they operate have taken different forms, the regional minister is a highly institutionalized element of the national cabinet (Bakvis 1991). Provincially, however, anything as formal and influential as Ottawa's system of regional political ministers is rarely in evidence, though powerful ministers with regional power bases are part of the political landscape and often take the lead in political and governmental matters affecting their regions. In research for this book, when asked explicitly about regional ministers, provincial ministers and political staff would either draw a blank or comment that they "thought" or "presumed" that X and Y were the key ministers in particular regions. No such uncertainty would be found in Ottawa.

The different nature of intergovernmental relations, broadly defined, is also of moment in comparing provincial and federal first ministers. The federal government's responsibility for international relations involves the prime minister in dealings with foreign countries, whereas the provinces have constitutional responsibility for municipal governments. The issues are obviously different, but more important are the very different exchange relations involved. Municipal politicians, beholden to their province for grants and approvals (and susceptible to all manner of interference, up to and including their legal elimination), have few effective bargaining chips in their dealings with the provinces, yet their concerns are of immediate political and electoral import to cabinet. Precisely the reverse is true for the federal government in its dealings with foreign countries. Moreover, prime ministers are wont to reserve interesting and important international relations responsibilities for themselves, whereas premiers by choice and necessity tend to remain aloof from most provincial-municipal issues.

An important difference between federal and provincial cabinets lies in the willingness of the latter to experiment. Even such seeming heresies as British Columbia's televising cabinet meetings do not fundamentally challenge the basic model of responsible government, but rather tinker with structures and processes. Other obvious examples include marginal or sometimes wholesale involvement of the government caucus or of individual backbenchers in cabinet decision making, and institutionalized cabinet tours and meetings outside the capital. Scale and complexity, which can easily lead to institutional inertia, may play a role in discouraging experimentation with cabinet structure and process in Ottawa, but attitudes are also important. Provincial politicians simply seem less averse to changing established cabinet institutions than do their Ottawa counterparts. Whether this stems from greater reverence in Ottawa for the accepted order, perhaps in turn reflecting greater influence from conservative officials, or from idiosyncratic quirks of provincial politics and political culture is an intriguing question.

Consensus Government in Nunavut and the Northwest Territories

If Canadian first ministers ever were *primus inter pares* within cabinet, they clearly are not today – save in the territorial North. Nunavut and the Northwest Territories adhere to an unusual variation of the

Westminster system, styled "consensus government," in which the premier's powers are sharply constrained. And while the prospects of Ottawa or the provinces adopting the principles and practices of consensus government are nil, no democratic audit of Canadian cabinets would be complete without reference to governance in the territories. Consensus government also serves as a concrete demonstration that the British cabinet-parliamentary system can be highly flexible and that it need not entail either a worrisome concentration of power or an autocratic first minister.

Many academics and practitioners reject out of hand the proposition that a Westminster system can exist without political parties, but all the essential constitutional principles of British-style responsible government – cabinet solidarity, ministerial responsibility, the centrality of parliamentary confidence in the government – are followed faithfully in consensus government. Political parties, however, are nowhere to be seen; candidates, including incumbent MLAs and ministers, seek election (and re-election) as independents. It would be wrong to assume that consensus government is simply a transitory stage of development, signifying lack of political maturity. Consensus government has held sway for two decades in the Northwest Territories and appears firmly established in Nunavut. Although it has its share of skeptics and critics, it also enjoys substantial popular support. One intriguing interpretation holds that consensus government reflects, or is at least congruent with, central tenets of traditional Northern Aboriginal political culture (White 1991; 2001).

Though unique in modern-day Canadian politics, consensus government in the northern territories bears a family resemblance to other Westminster systems in small jurisdictions. Several former British protectorates in the South Pacific, such as Fiji, Tuvalu, and Vanuatu, developed Westminster-style cabinet-parliamentary systems that lack political parties and reflect the influence of Aboriginal cultural norms (Lynch 1982). Similarly, the Isle of Man, a semi-independent British Crown dependency in the Irish Sea, is governed by a council of ministers responsible to Tynwald, the ancient Manx parliament, members of which are elected on a nonparty basis (Kermode 2002).

Without the backing of disciplined political parties, in the northern consensus system cabinet effectively operates as a permanent minority government, with private members wielding unusual influence. Just as the cabinet is unable to dominate the legislature like its southern counterparts, so too the premier cannot exercise the same control over cabinet as other Canadian first ministers do. The key to all this is the process for selecting cabinet. Whereas first ministers "south of sixty" are determined – albeit indirectly – by the voters and enjoy unquestioned authority to pick and choose ministers, under consensus government the premier and the cabinet are chosen by secret ballot of all MLAs following each election. The premier assigns ministers to portfolios, shuffles them, and may, though only in the most extraordinary circumstances, remove them from office, but ultimately ministers are beholden to the MLAs rather than to the premier for their cabinet posts. Important tools are available to the premier, such as the authority to hire, fire, and shuffle deputy ministers, and she or he is clearly the leader of the government and its pre-eminent figure. Nevertheless, the premier's control over cabinet as a group and over ministers individually is sharply constrained. The premier must lead by dint of inspiration, persuasion, hard work, and experience, not through raw power.

The limits on the first minister's power are illustrated in two recent cases involving the removal of ministers from office. In 2003 Jack Anawak, a minister in the Nunavut cabinet, spoke out strongly against a cabinet decision that stood to adversely affect his riding. When he refused Premier Paul Okalik's direction to abide by cabinet solidarity, Okalik's only recourse was to strip Anawak of his portfolios. Although Nunavut's Legislative Assembly and Executive Council Act (SNu 2002, c. 5, s.66[2]) proclaims that ministers serve at the pleasure of the premier, Okalik thought that since the Assembly had voted Anawak into cabinet, he lacked authority to remove him. Anawak refused to resign but was formally ousted by the MLAs who had put him in office. More recently, Henry Zoe's position as an NWT minister came into question for comments he had allegedly made in a Yellowknife bar about Newfoundlanders. Premier Joe Handley took away Zoe's portfolios, but told the Assembly, "I don't have the authority to remove a Minister," recommending that the MLAs decide whether Zoe should remain one (NWT Legislative Assembly 2004, 1328). The MLAs voted him out of cabinet.

As these intriguing insights into consensus government suggest, the premier and the cabinet live under constant threat of removal by the MLAs. Nor is this a theoretical possibility: both ministers and premiers (called "government leaders" until the early 1990s) have been, in the evocative local phraseology, "taken out" by the legislature. Although infrequent, this has occurred either when individual ministers found themselves in increasingly serious political trouble (some resign to escape the ignominy of formal censure) or through the mechanism of the midterm review. This formal, extended accountability session for cabinet at the halfway mark of the electoral cycle can culminate in proceedings to remove ministers from office. Though ministers normally escape midterm reviews with nothing more serious than a public dressing-down from the MLAs, the threat of dismissal from office is ever-present. And yet, both in the Northwest Territories and Nunavut, MLAs frequently complain that they are ignored by cabinet, that consensus government is a sham, and that ministers are arrogant and unaccountable in their exercise of power. Whether such criticisms are well founded is not the point here; they demonstrate that even in settings most favourable to making cabinet responsive, charges of untoward, uncontrolled concentration of power in cabinet figure prominently in the political landscape (O'Brien 2003; White 2004).

At the same time, critics attack consensus government from the opposite direction. Cabinet is said to lack coherence and discipline and to be preoccupied with log-rolling on capital projects. One knowledgeable critic dismissed the NWT cabinet as little more than a body that "casts lots for the use of the large federal transfers which make up the NWT budget" (Jull 1991, 54). Failings are often attributed to the premier's weak position vis-à-vis cabinet, and of course to the absence of political parties. In short, the concern is that the premier lacks the capacity to be sufficiently autocratic. Both territories have toyed with the idea of moving to a hybrid system that would see the premier popularly elected on a territory-wide basis. Such a change would certainly enhance the premier's power, though it would of course mark the end of British-style responsible government.

Canadian Cabinets: Variation and Change

No great point would be served in summarizing what in itself is a summary of the principal features of Canadian cabinets and core executives. A few points, however, bear highlighting.

First and foremost, while the underlying constitutional principles are clear and invariant – such as the need for the government to retain the confidence of the elected members and cabinet solidarity – they by no means entail a single orthodox model of cabinet organization and operation. Even aside from the consensus governments of the North, variations are evident across Canada. As well, on several important dimensions, Canadian practices stand out as distinct from those of other Anglo-Celtic Westminster systems. It follows that the scope for change is considerable; many possibilities exist for altering cabinet and core executive while remaining faithful to essential responsible government principles.

Moreover, while key central structures and principles of the core executive endure much as they were in the nineteenth century, others have undergone substantial transformation, especially in the past few decades. These range from the highly institutionalized, such as the rise of central agencies and cabinet committees, to the addition of new political structures, such as ministers' personal staff, to informal political practices, such as the increased frequency of cabinet shuffles. Whether these changes have enhanced or detracted from democracy is the question we now turn to, beginning with the charge that Canadian first ministers have become little more than elected dictators.

CHAPTER 2

- Cabinet government in Canada operates on the basis of Westminster (responsible government) principles shared with other Anglo-Celtic democracies, such as Great Britain, Ireland, Australia, and New Zealand.

- Within the broad Westminster family of democratic systems, Canada exhibits a number of distinctive or unique features.

- A key and distinctive element in the construction of Canadian cabinets is the representational imperative: the principle that important regional, cultural, social, and economic interests should have representatives at the cabinet table.

- Cabinets collectively, and ministers individually, have extensive advisory and operational staff support, including permanent bureaucratic officials and partisan political staff.

- Though they follow the same basic constitutional precepts, federal and provincial cabinets exhibit significant structural and operational variations, reflecting both scale and the differing nature of federal and provincial politics.

- The unique consensus governments in Nunavut and the Northwest Territories are true Westminster systems, characterized by very different power relationships among first minister, cabinet, and noncabinet members than are found "south of sixty."

3 THE FIRST MINISTER AS AUTOCRAT?

A central question about democracy in this country is whether first ministers exercise dictatorial power over Canadian governments by virtue of unchallenged control over what is at least nominally a collective decision-making body – cabinet. The implications of this question go far beyond issues of internal cabinet democracy, extending to the essential nature of our political system. Certainly the conventional wisdom portrays the Canadian prime minister and his provincial counterparts as extraordinarily powerful, easily eclipsing their cabinets. Journalist Jeffrey Simpson's recent book, *The friendly dictatorship*, is very much in this tradition, arguing as it does that Canadian politics are characterized by "the massive centralization of power in one man's control within the trappings of a parliamentary system" (Simpson 2001, xi).

This chapter addresses the power of the first minister. In terms of the audit benchmarks set out in Chapter 1, the issue of the first minister's role in cabinet is essentially one of participation. Do ministers truly participate in decision making? Has the first minister usurped cabinet's decision-making prerogatives? In addition, another of the principal audit criteria is directly relevant: accountability and transparency. Often the criticism is not so much that power is concentrated in one person's hands as that unelected advisors around the first minister wield great influence in a secretive and unaccountable manner.

Outside the upper echelons of government, few know who these people are or what they do. Moreover, although ministers are powerful, they are publicly held to account for their actions, through Question Period, in the media, and by the people come election time. Not so, the argument runs, for those in the backrooms. That these staff are directly accountable to the first minister is at best a partial rebuttal given the concern that they may be pursuing their own agendas while claiming to act in the first minister's name.

In Britain, it has been argued that the debate, which reaches back to the 1960s, over the extent and the merits of prime ministerial government is ultimately sterile and unproductive and that there are more analytically useful ways of looking at power relationships within the core executive (Smith 2000). This argument is doubtless also valid in Canada. Yet the elemental importance of the first minister's power for questions of democracy cannot be denied. Hence this chapter begins with a summary of the most sophisticated account of prime ministerial government in Canada, Donald Savoie's *Governing from the centre*, and then considers some of the constraints on that power and the context in which it is exercised. Following this is a discussion of the thesis that provincial government is premiers' government. After a brief review of some of the unique or unusual features of the Canadian political system that impinge on the power of the first minister, the "first minister as autocrat" argument is examined.

At the risk of giving the game away and having readers skip to Chapter 4, the overall thrust here is that although Canadian first ministers are indeed singularly powerful, they fall short of autocracy. Fears that our political system has descended into a dictatorship (friendly or otherwise) are not borne out.

Governing from the Centre

The prime minister as autocrat interpretation of Canadian politics, as Herman Bakvis (2001) terms it, is hardly new. More than thirty years ago, Denis Smith's well-known paper (1977), "President and Parliament," argued that Pierre Trudeau had transformed the office of prime minister – and with it Canadian politics – by instituting a series of presidential practices without the checks and balances that limit executive power in the United States. Donald Savoie (1999) contends that the concentration of power at the centre has markedly intensified since Smith wrote. Even a skeptic like Bakvis, who raises incisive questions about the prime minister as autocrat argument, nonetheless describes it as "simultaneously compelling and disturbing" (Bakvis 2001, 64).

Savoie is no ivory tower academic, speculating from afar about the exercise of power. His background includes a stint as a ministerial assistant, service as a senior bureaucrat, intimate involvement in the 1993 Liberal transition, and extensive interaction with prominent Ottawa politicians and mandarins. He builds a case at once nuanced and thorough, identifying a range of developments that have contributed to enhancing the centre's power. He points, for example, to the increasingly multidimensional character of problems and policies that prevents their easy allocation into discrete departmental realms, with the result that "many more issues or files will fall to the prime minister's in-basket" (Savoie 1999, 11).

At root, Savoie's argument rests on the substantial expansion in the size, scope, and influence of the political-bureaucratic apparatus supporting the prime minister, primarily the Prime Minister's Office (PMO) and the Privy Council Office (PCO). Until the late 1960s, the clerk of the Privy Council was first and foremost the cabinet secretary, and his staff focused on cabinet work. The clerk has now essentially become deputy minister to the prime minister, with the PCO staff principally oriented to serving the prime minister (Savoie 1999, 113-14). Tellingly, for instance, some PCO briefing materials are prepared for the exclusive use of the prime minister. In addition, the central agencies have come to assume a substantial operational role, intruding into what was once the exclusive purview of the line departments (320). Standing as both cause and effect of these developments are the recurring cuts imposed by the central agencies on the departments – cuts from which the centre largely exempted itself. As well, changes in the career paths of deputy ministers have effectively enfolded deputy ministers into the centre: modern-day deputies typically have extensive central agency experience and are shuffled too frequently to develop long-term departmental ties (302). Indeed, major shuffles of deputy ministers are now conventionally interpreted as reflections of the prime minister's plans and priorities (Winsor 2002). Savoie also points out that not only is the PMO large, but, unusually for Westminster systems, senior staff positions are held exclusively by partisans. Since politicos naturally owe their loyalty to the prime minister, whereas bureaucrats are more inclined to uphold the interests of the government as a whole, this enhances the prime minister's power (Savoie 1999, 101).

Some seasoned Ottawa watchers maintain that Savoie's focus on the policy- and decision-making process causes him to underestimate the degree of power concentrated at the centre. The centre's control over government communications and "issues management" – the polite term for political firefighting – is even more pronounced, they say, than its sway over the routine policy process. This control is tied to the influence of the pollsters and media spin doctors at the prime minister's service through the PMO and the government party (which Savoie incorporates into his argument).

Savoie does recognize that important constraints circumscribe the prime minister's power. The prime minister, for example, faces serious overload problems and can focus on only a few key issues (Savoie 1999, 8). Moreover – and especially germane to our concerns – no prime minister can afford to run roughshod over his ministers repeatedly: "The prime minister's summary and decision on his definition of the Cabinet consensus cannot always go blatantly against the sense of the meeting if he is to retain the confidence of his ministers" (86). Yet the prime minister can and does impose his will on cabinet; as Savoie observes, "The prime minister has access to virtually all the necessary levers in Cabinet to ensure that he or she is the 'boss' in Cabinet, and that if he so wishes – and prime ministers usually do – he can dominate Cabinet deliberations and its decision making" (81). In addition, all recent prime ministers have embarked on major policy initiatives without so much as consulting cabinet or even the responsible minister.

The Prime Minister's Power: Context and Constraints

Paul Thomas, a leading academic analyst of Canada's governmental institutions, suggests that portrayals of prime ministers as friendly dictators and cabinet as focus group are "good rhetoric, but poor analysis" (Thomas 2003-4, 80). While recognizing the inherently centralized power of cabinet-parliamentary government, Thomas contends that the constraints on prime ministerial power are substantial and that power in the core executive is relational, flowing in complex patterns among key players – primarily, but not exclusively, the first minister and the cabinet.

Savoie (1999) develops his argument primarily in terms of changes internal to government, such as the evolving role of senior bureaucrats, the growth of central agencies, and shifts in the resources and options available to ministers. As Bakvis points out, however, the power and position of the prime minister must be understood in broader, systemic terms. A good deal of what appears to be prime ministerial autocracy, for example, may be better thought of as a reflection of the one-party dominance characteristic of national Canadian politics. Similarly, Canadian first ministers' unusual capacity to dominate their cabinets and caucuses stems in substantial measure from Canadian political parties' leadership selection and removal processes. At the same time, the imperatives of federalism impose very significant restrictions that must be reckoned into any overall assessment of prime ministerial power (Bakvis 2001).

Bakvis (2001) questions Savoie's claims about growing concentration of power at the centre, noting that prime ministers as far back as John A. Macdonald and Wilfrid Laurier exercised strong control over their parties and ministers. He further argues that throughout Canadian history, cabinet has either been bypassed altogether or asked to render essentially pro forma decisions on important policy matters that had been effectively settled by the prime minister and the responsible minister. Such criticisms do not dispute the concentration of power at the centre but rather arguments that it is of recent provenance.

For our purposes – assessing the degree of democracy at the pinnacle of the governmental decision-making process – the question is whether power has shifted from cabinet collectively to the prime minister or to individual ministers. In a direct confrontation of one of Savoie's central points, Bakvis reinterprets his evidence that cabinet is doing much less (in terms of number of meetings, documents considered, and decisions rendered) to suggest that Prime Minister Chrétien shifted power from cabinet to individual ministers rather than to himself. Bakvis contends that Chrétien "meddled remarkably little" in major portfolios, leaving ministers with "considerable latitude," though he acknowledges that this trend underscores "the main point of Savoie's 1999 book, namely that cabinet as a collective, corporate body has become much less relevant, even if certain individual ministers still enjoy influence" (Bakvis 2001, 66).

A departmentalized cabinet, in which ministers individually rather than cabinet collectively predominate, is hardly equivalent to a cabinet bereft of power because everything is run from the centre. By the explicit design of his cabinet and by the clear signals he sent, Chrétien expressly empowered his ministers. Journalists Edward Greenspon and Anthony Wilson-Smith's account of the first Chrétien mandate is unequivocal:

> Chrétien was a big believer in giving ministers their head. He liked to tell the story of how Trudeau had once taken him aside and asked "Jean, are you mad at me? You haven't spoken to me for a long time." Chrétien replied that everything was fine, he was just doing his job. "My job is not to be a bother." That was Chrétien's model of a good minister; one who didn't bother the prime minister ... Chrétien had resented the manner in which the Prime Minister's Office and the Privy Council Office had

dominated ministers in the Trudeau years and, so much the product of his personal experiences, would refrain from doing the same (Greenspon and Wilson-Smith 1996, 161, 163).

Savoie acknowledges that the number and complexity of issues requiring attention constrain the first minister (and by extension, those around him or her), but may not have accorded this fact the significance it deserves. Based on his experience as Trudeau's principal secretary, Tom Axworthy argues strongly that the only way a modern-day prime minister can accomplish anything of note is to focus on a handful of key issues and delegate everything else to ministers. Neither the prime minister – even one as intellectually able as Trudeau – nor the staff of the PMO – "whatever the pretensions or even the ambitions of its inhabitants, the Prime Minister's Office in Canada is not the White House North" (Axworthy 1988, 249) – has the capacity to take charge of more than a small proportion of the important and pressing matters before government, let alone the mundane and routine ones. Thomas agrees: "Sharing the burden of running government necessarily means sharing power. Departmental ministers carry on the great bulk of government programmes with little or no direction from the Prime Minister" (Thomas 2003-4, 81).

As Savoie has documented, and others have long observed, central agencies have greatly expanded in size and capacity over the past few decades (both federally and provincially). Yet in important ways Canadian first ministers and the political-bureaucratic apparatus supporting them are *less* capable of dominating government than was the case before the days of expansive central agencies. The reasons for this are many and varied. Substantial growth in the scale of government (even with the cutbacks, privatizations, and downsizing of the last decade and more), together with the increasingly complex nature of public policy, simply renders it impossible for any one person to oversee an entire government or to be well versed on anything like the range of important issues facing modern-day governments. Strong central agencies diminish but can never overcome this problem. And as Axworthy (1988) reminds us, even the Prime Minister's Office has relatively few political operatives; most staff answer phones and letters. Canadian political culture has also shifted to become notably more demanding of transparency, inclusiveness, and consultation in public policy processes. As well, the past few decades have witnessed palpable increases in the number and influence of institutional counterweights to the first minister and the central agencies: far more aggressive and knowledgeable media, complex networks of active and politically astute interest groups, and better educated, more professional, and less docile MPs.

In Ottawa, at least, central agencies have certainly grown in size and scope even as government – measured both in terms of staff complement and number of agencies and departments – has shrunk. But at the same time, both the rhetoric and the reality of modern-day governance emphasize the importance of coordination (called "horizontality," or in the UK, "joined-up government"). The increasing interdependence of policies and departments, not to mention their intergovernmental and international elements, render the task of coordination especially difficult and time consuming (Thomas 2003-4). Otherwise put, a good deal of central agencies' time and effort is necessarily devoted to simply dealing with coordination, which is rather different from exercising control.

Finally, while the power of the central agencies is undoubted, the argument that the clout and expertise of central agencies dramatically enhance the first minister's dominance may be questioned on both logical and empirical grounds. The unspoken assumption here is that the various central agencies constitute a formidable, monolithic administrative machine backing the first minister. The (small-p) political reality is that central agencies can be rivals for power and influence and that the first minister may well encounter conflict and dissension among his or her central agents, and thus not support and strength, but weakness and division.

The typically powerful position of the finance minister represents another weakness in the first minister as autocrat thesis. (Of course, if one takes a wide reading of "the centre" to include this pivotal figure, the "governing from the centre" interpretation is strengthened.) Finance ministers are rarely less than a formidable force in Canadian cabinets. For all Prime Minister Chrétien's misgivings about archrival Paul Martin's ambitions, during most of their uneasy partnership, he consistently and unambiguously supported Martin's initiatives and afforded him extensive leeway in the critically important area of economic and fiscal policy (Greenspon and Wilson-Smith 1996). It is a firmly established principle in Canadian governments (federal, provincial, and territorial) that although the first minister may influence its overall direction and occasionally prescribe specific provisions, the budget – in many ways the government's central policy instrument – is essentially the finance minister's preserve. In terms of cabinet democracy, it may well be cause for concern that, as many cabinet insiders have observed, the combination of a determined finance minister and a supportive first minister is all but unbeatable in cabinet, but this is a rather different question.

In a recent revisiting of his earlier work, Savoie reiterates the heightened political-bureaucratic resources available to the prime minister, but also emphasizes the role of the media with their increasing focus on party leaders, the prime minister's extensive network of media advisors and pollsters, and his or her unassailable position as party leader, deriving from the supine (not his word) nature of the parliamentary caucus (Savoie forthcoming). These arguments carry substantial force, yet are less clear-cut than might first appear. In terms of the first minister's phalanx of spin doctors and media professionals, what has been said of Australia applies equally to Canada: "Contemporary Australian prime ministers now find that the speechwriters, public opinion pollsters, press secretaries and media experts become an indispensable part of their personal staff simply because that aspect of their job has become so much more significant in the television age" (Hart 1992, 194). The demands of the media are relentless; not only are media more intrusive and aggressive but they expect immediate responses from political leaders 24-7. (Consider that during the massive August 2003 blackout of eastern North America, Prime Minister Chrétien and Premier Eves of Ontario were roundly criticized for allowing several *hours* to elapse before making themselves available for media conferences and photo ops.) In short, first ministers require far more extensive media staff than their predecessors just to keep from losing ground.

According to Savoie, it is "unthinkable" that a Canadian caucus might depose a sitting prime minister, as has occurred in Britain and Australia; "Even at the depths of [Prime Minister] Mulroney's unpopularity," he notes, "there was no indication that his caucus was about to boot him out of office" (Savoie forthcoming). Of course, Canadian caucuses lack both the formal power and the process for deposing party leaders, though as discussed below, caucuses may be able to make their life sufficiently difficult that leaders quit of their own accord. While the definitive account of Prime Minister Chrétien's decision to retire will be some time coming, it is certainly thinkable that Liberal caucus discontent following Finance Minister Paul Martin's dismissal in June 2002 substantially contributed to – indeed, forced – the prime minister's announcement of retirement. (Savoie's most recent discussion of prime ministerial government does not mention the Martin-Chrétien conflict and its implications for prime ministerial power.) As to the Tory caucus under Mulroney, its unwavering support of the often-embattled prime minister was due to the great pains Mulroney took to keep on good terms with his MPs, respecting their opinions and taking their concerns seriously (Laghi 2002). This is not to say that Prime Minister Mulroney turned over significant power to his backbenchers – he did not – but he certainly did not take them for granted and worked diligently at maintaining their support.

The forced resignation of Prime Minister Chrétien, the ouster of Canadian Alliance leader Stockwell Day, and the circumstances surrounding John Savage's departure from the Nova Scotia premiership have led scholars of both Parliament and political parties to conclude that, regardless of formal procedures for leadership review, the parliamentary party has the capacity to remove party leaders. As Bill Cross writes in his Democratic Audit volume, "Though the parties' constitutions no longer give the caucus this authority [to remove the leader], recent events suggest that leaders cannot continue for long without the support of their parliamentary party ... the political reality is that caucus holds the trump card in removing leaders ... the leadership cannot be maintained in the face of widespread caucus opposition" (Cross 2004, 104-5). Jonathan Malloy, a leading analyst of Canada's Parliament, concurs: "Having become more assertive and willing to carve out an expanded role for themselves, Members contributed clearly – and likely decisively – to the downfall of two key party leaders" (Malloy 2003, 69).

Provincial Government: Premiers' Government?

Savoie makes a strong case for prime ministerial autocracy in Ottawa, but what of the provinces? If, indeed, "provincial government is premier's government," does it not follow that provincial first ministers are even more autocratic than the prime minister? As discussed in Chapter 2, the argument that the provincial premier enjoys authority "significantly greater than that of his federal counterpart" (Young and Morley 1983, 54) turns on the much greater scale and complexity of national governance. This renders control by one person, even with the support of an extensive political-bureaucratic apparatus, significantly more problematic in Ottawa than at the provincial level.

A quarter-century earlier, J.R. Mallory reached a similar conclusion, declaring, "The position of the premier is notably stronger than in the federal cabinet." His reasoning followed a somewhat different path, though it did largely reduce to the less complex nature of provincial politics. Since regional representation was less pronounced in provincial cabinets, which were thus less subject to "sectional veto," provincial premiers encountered less "diffusion of power" in their cabinets. Moreover, the less generous salaries paid provincial ministers "produces, except among the few 'key' members of a government, a large group of clearly part-time ministers who cannot afford to forsake their private business affairs and who thereby sacrifice political influence in the cabinet" (Mallory 1956, 201).

In certain ways, recent developments have enhanced the premier's dominant position: larger and more powerful central agencies, for example, and changes in ministerial career patterns. As noted in the previous chapter, provincial cabinet ministers are shuffled with far greater abandon than was the case a few decades ago. While length of tenure is no guarantee of influence, the longer ministers remain in their portfolios, the more they learn about them and the greater portfolio-related political resources they accumulate, thus putting them in a stronger position vis-à-vis the premier.

Other changes have worked in the opposite direction. For example, with reference to one of Mallory's arguments, although salaries of provincial ministers still lag behind those of their federal counter-parts, they are at least sufficient to obviate the need for ministers to moonlight to make ends meet. The demands of the job are such that there can be few if any part-time ministers left in Canada.

Accounts of highly autocratic premiers who operated as "one-man bands," such as Joey Smallwood in Newfoundland, W.A.C. Bennett in British Columbia, and Leslie Frost in Ontario, offer strong confirmation of the thesis that provincial government is premiers' government. Yet the names of these notably dominant premiers mean little to most Canadians under forty, since they held sway in the 1950s and 1960s. Few, if any, of their successors have enjoyed the unfettered power they wielded. In large measure, this reflects the changes in the context of Canadian politics over the past few decades listed earlier, such as growth in the scale and complexity of governance and more potent interest groups.

Provincial premiers may wield extraordinary powers well beyond what any prime minister could normally call upon. Two recent Ontario illustrations underline the point. Premier Mike Harris's desire to give the province's professional sports teams a tax break offers a remarkable glimpse of raw premierial power. Following a heated but indecisive debate in cabinet, in his final days in office, Harris had an order in council prepared and "walked around" to pliant ministers who signed the secret document. The finance minister, who vehemently opposed the idea, was out of the country at the time and later stated publicly, "I did not support a change in the policy ... I would not have signed it had it been presented to me" – though only after an unholy uproar had arisen and it was clear that the new premier did not support the tax break (Jim Flaherty quoted in Benzie 2002; Mallan 2002).

Following Harris's retirement in early 2002, Ernie Eves served as premier until a crushing electoral defeat in the fall of 2003. According to *Toronto Star* reporter Thomas Walkom, Eves's short time in office was marked by extraordinary usurpation of cabinet prerogatives by the Premier's Office (it is worth noting that Walkom is no sensationalist muckraker but a respected journalist with impeccable academic credentials). Walkom writes of Eves's tenure:

> Cabinet was rarely consulted about decisions. Indeed the inner cabinet, the powerful planning and priorities board, never met at all after Eves took the helm.
>
> "Ernie hated debating things in cabinet," explained one Queen's Park insider. "He preferred making these decisions with one or two close advisers over steak at Bigliardi's [a pricey Toronto restaurant]."
>
> In some cases, ministers found out only through the press that they had agreed to spend millions of dollars on this or that project (Walkom 2003).

A central element in Eves's exclusion of cabinet ministers from key decisions was what amounted to a parallel finance ministry in the Premier's Office, run by a former deputy minister of finance. This operation "squeezed the real finance ministry – and its minister, Janet Ecker – right out of the game ... 'the budget was drafted in the office of the premier,' said [a senior Tory]. 'He [Eves] put in what he wanted and passed it over to Janet to announce'" (Walkom 2003). The politically catastrophic decision to present the budget at an auto parts facility rather than in the Legislature (the so-called Magna budget) was taken in the Premier's Office without consulting Ecker (Urquhart 2003b).

That the Eves government was marked by terminal disarray and suffered accordingly at the polls is not the key point here. Such usurpation of ministerial authority – individual and collective – is hard to imagine on a similar scale in Ottawa. And if a premier could finesse formal processes to this extent in Canada's largest province, what might transpire in smaller jurisdictions, where the possibilities for premiers to centralize power in their offices are even greater?

Provincial government is indeed premiers' government.

Canadian Exceptionalism

By their very nature, parliamentary systems in the British style are characterized by powerful executives led by dominant first ministers. In considering the question of cabinet democracy in Canada, though, it is well to recognize that even by Westminster standards, Canadian first ministers wield exceptional power. Their unusually strong position reflects both unique Canadian institutional arrangements, such as leadership selection processes, and the absence of institutional constraints found in other British cabinet-parliamentary systems.

Compared with their counterparts in Britain, Australia, New Zealand, and Ireland, Canadian first ministers are all but impervious to cabinet or caucus revolts by virtue of the leadership selection processes in Canadian political parties. Canadian party leaders are selected by much more broadly based processes than are leaders in the other Anglo-Celtic parliamentary systems, who are chosen by the parliamentary parties (in Canadian parlance, caucus). The British Conservative Party is a recent and only partial exception, and at the time of writing, Fine Gael, one of Ireland's main parties, was deciding whether to adopt a membership-based leadership selection process. In Canada, either large conventions of party activists or the party membership en masse elect party leaders. Thus prime ministers cannot be removed as party leaders by their cabinets or caucuses – as happened most famously to Margaret Thatcher in Britain (1990), and also to Bob Hawke in Australia (1991), Charles Haughey in Ireland (1992), and James Bolger in New Zealand (1997) – for the very good reason that these groups did not choose them in the first place. Otherwise put, Canadian first ministers are insulated from political pressure from cabinet to a degree unknown in other Westminster systems. Although Prime Minister Chrétien's departure was affected by pressure from his party and his caucus, he nonetheless left on his own terms and at the time of his choosing.

Paradoxically, the move toward democratization of party leadership selection and removal procedures, by turning the decision over to tens of thousands of party members rather than a couple of thousand convention delegates – let alone a caucus of a few dozen – has compromised the overall quality of Canadian democracy. The net result has been to "exacerbate the problem of leader domination in Canadian politics ... by diminishing the effective power of elected caucus members and giving formal power to relatively inactive and unorganized party members, 'democratic' leadership selection actually increases the political distance between political leaders and the people" (Bateman 2001, 21-2).

A corollary of Canadian first ministers being less subject to removal by their parliamentary caucuses is their greater capacity to fire ministers. Though first ministers uniformly say that dismissing ministers ranks among the worst duties they have to perform, their political power to do so is unquestioned and they do not flinch from dumping ministers when need be. In contrast, the Australian prime minister rarely sacks ministers: over a twenty-five-year stretch only one Australian minister was removed from office "simply because he was not up to the job," though others fell victim to personal errors or to decisions of their party factions, and of course ministers resigned for a variety of reasons. Ultimately, though, "it has been rare for the prime minister to initiate such actions" (Weller 1992b, 22).

The contrast between Canada and other Westminster systems in this respect is starkly encapsulated in two episodes. In 1962 British prime minister Harold Macmillan dumped six of twenty-two cabinet ministers, an extraordinary event that continues to figure prominently in the lore of British politics as "the night of the long knives." On taking power as prime minister, Paul Martin fired no fewer than twenty-three of Jean Chrétien's thirty-eight ministers. Naturally this move excited considerable attention, but the principal interest was in whether it would improve or harm the prime minister's political standing, not in the staggering exercise of power itself.

Rather less crucial than party leadership selection processes, though still an important institutional enhancement of the first minister's position, is the formal role of the first minister as party leader in approving candidates for Parliament and the provincial and territorial legislatures. Under federal election law, as well as in Nova Scotia, New Brunswick, Quebec, Saskatchewan, and the Yukon, a candidate may run under a party label only if the party leader signs the nomination forms. In other provinces, the party leader plays no official role in the required party authorization, though he or she usually controls the party machinery tightly (Blake 2001, table 5). Though refusal of a party leader to sign a putative candidate's nomination papers is unusual, it is not unknown. The threat that a first minister will veto a candidacy, especially that of a sitting MP or MLA, is a blunt and unpalatable tool for quashing dissent, but the power is nonetheless real. So too is the power held by some Canadian party leaders to override local nomination processes and unilaterally impose a candidate on a local riding association, regardless of its wishes. Another significant exercise of the first minister's power as party leader was Prime Minister Chrétien's effective proscription of nomination challenges against sitting Liberal MPs. (When he became Liberal leader, Prime Minister Martin abandoned this practice, but reinstated it when faced with the uncertainties of minority government.)

Again, the contrast with other Anglo-Celtic parliamentary systems is stark. In the UK, Australia, Ireland, and New Zealand, first ministers are obviously influential within their parties, but nominations are the preserve of local and regional party organizations. By and large, in these countries first ministers (including at the state level in Australia) and national party organizations lack the capacity that their Canadian counterparts enjoy to control or veto local nomination processes (Denver 1998; Galligan 1999; C. Sharman, personal communication, 2 May 2002).

A recent change to federal electoral law portends even greater control by party leaders over party matters, with obvious implications for the power of the prime minister. Local constituency associations wishing to be formally registered with Elections Canada (important for legal and financial reasons) must be endorsed by the party leader, who can in effect de-register a local constituency association with the support of only two party officials (Winsor 2003). To say the least, this is a handy power for quelling potential party revolts and for controlling the party organization.

Canadian first ministers are also exempt from practices that constrain their counterparts in other Anglo-Celtic systems. In Australia and New Zealand, for example, Labor prime ministers are not free to choose their cabinets, but must accept the choices emerging from caucus elections. The status that caucus election confers on ministers also limits prime ministers in exercising their right to dismiss ministers. These constraints are less onerous than might first appear (typically the caucus choices differ only marginally from those an unfettered prime minister might have made), but are nonetheless real.

Measuring first ministers' power in any systematic way is all but impossible, but some quantitative indicators can be suggestive. Tables 3.1, 3.2, and 3.3 present data on first ministers in Anglo-Celtic Westminster systems over roughly the period since the Second World War. Table 3.1 summarizes the reasons prime ministers in Australia, Canada, Ireland, New Zealand, and the UK left office. Canadian prime ministers left office either by choice – they retired – or because they were defeated at the polls. Elsewhere, however, retirement and electoral defeat were by no means the only causes of a prime minister's

Table 3.1

Reasons prime ministers left office, 1939-2003

	Died in office	Retired	Lost election*	Lost confidence vote	Ousted by party
Australia**	2	1	4	1	5
Canada	0	5	6	0	0
Ireland	1	2	9	2	2
New Zealand	0	3	8	0	2
United Kingdom	0	3	7	0	2

 * Includes instances in which loss of confidence vote led to an election.
** One instance of a PM dismissed by governor general not included in any column.
Source: Biographical data on government websites.

departure. Remarkably, in Australia, more prime ministers were removed from office by their own parties than by the voters. British, Irish, and New Zealand prime ministers also suffered the ignominy of being ousted by their parties, but no modern Canadian prime minister has met that fate.

Tables 3.2 and 3.3 look at length of time in office of national prime ministers and of state or provincial premiers in Australia and Canada (the other three countries are not federal). At both national and sub-national levels, Canadian first ministers' mean length of service is longer than elsewhere. (It is fair to add that including the twenty-one years in office of the remarkable Irish taoiseach Eamon De Valera would have raised the mean for Irish first ministers to 5.1 years.) Even more telling is the unusually large number of Canadian first ministers

Table 3.2

Prime ministers' tenure in office

Country	Years	Number*	Mean years in office	Years in office <2	2.0-4.9	5.0-9.9	10+
Australia	1939-2004	15	4.3	6	5	3	1
Canada	1935-2003	11	5.5	3	2	3	3
Ireland	1948-2004	14	4.0	4	5	5	0
New Zealand	1940-2004	15	4.3	7	2	5	1
UK	1940-2004	13	4.9	2	6	4	1

* Prime ministers who returned to office after leaving, such as Churchill, Trudeau, and Menzies, are counted twice.
Source: Biographical data on government websites.

Table 3.3

State or provincial premiers' tenure in office

Country	Number	Mean years in office	Years in office <2 (%)	2.0-4.9 (%)	5.0-9.9 (%)	10+ (%)
Australian states	84	4.5	38	23	29	11
Canadian provinces	94	6.4	29	12	34	26

Source: Biographical data on government websites.

who remained in office for over a decade. As many Canadian prime ministers (King, Trudeau, and Chrétien) enjoyed more than ten consecutive years in power as in the other four countries combined. More than half of Canada's prime ministers remained in office for over five years, compared with barely a third of first ministers in the other countries. At the state-provincial level, more than twice as many Canadian as Australian premiers had a ten-year run or longer; 60 percent of Canadian premiers but only 40 percent of their antipodean counterparts lasted six or more years atop the greasy pole.

The data in the tables suggest that so long as they remain electorally successful, Canadian first ministers have a far firmer lock on power than first ministers in other Anglo-Celtic Westminster systems. The data clearly confirm the relative longevity of Canadian first ministers. This is significant since the longer a prime minister or premier remains in office, the more entrenched and dominant he or she is likely to become. In short, the data reinforce the conclusion that Canadian first ministers are exceptionally powerful even by Westminster standards.

To be sure, Canadian first ministers face political restrictions on their power that either do not exist or are notably less inhibiting in other systems. The countervailing power of the provinces within the Canadian federal system, the wide-ranging limitations imposed by the Charter of Rights and Freedoms, and the constraints on cabinet composition imposed by the representational imperative somewhat counterbalance Canadian first ministers' unusually dominant position. Overall, though, Canadian first ministers wield qualitatively greater power than prime ministers and premiers in Britain, New Zealand, Australia, and Ireland.

Defining Autocracy

Assessing just how autocratic Canadian first ministers are in dealing with their cabinets collectively and their ministers individually is a bit of a mug's game. Establishing anything like precise criteria is fraught with difficulty. Is a first minister who routinely accepts cabinet decisions, even when they run counter to her preferences, but who occasionally imposes a unilateral decision against cabinet's wishes or without its knowledge, an autocrat? If not, how many times, and on what kind of issues, must a first minister overrule cabinet or bypass it entirely to qualify as an autocrat? Is a first minister who listens carefully to ministers' arguments but ultimately chooses to proceed against what would otherwise seem the cabinet consensus an autocrat? What of first ministers who get their way not by explicit exercise of power but through shrewdness, superior intellect, or hard work?

Let us offer the following, admittedly inexact, criteria. Autocratic first ministers are those who routinely impose important decisions against the clear will of cabinet; who repeatedly take significant actions without consulting cabinet, cabinet committees, or the responsible ministers; who intervene (either personally or through staff) in day-to-day departmental operations or decisions; who sanction staff (political or bureaucratic) to issue decrees on important policy matters to ministers or departments; and who respond to criticism or opposition from cabinet colleagues with threats or retribution. It might be objected that requiring such extreme behaviour to qualify as autocratic amounts to setting up an easily demolished straw man, for no Canadian first minister is *that* dictatorial. Perhaps so, but this set of measures is nonetheless useful as a benchmark. Identifying the occasional episode in which a first minister acts in an imperious manner is by no means confirmation that he or she is consistently and fundamentally autocratic. If, to recast a phrase, all first ministers are autocratic some of the time but no first ministers are autocratic all of the time, having at least general criteria helps us focus what we mean by "autocratic first ministers."

We then confront the problem of amassing and judging the evidence (largely drawn from interviews with provincial politicians, bureaucrats, and premiers; see appendix, p. 189). We cannot hope to have anything more than the most perfunctory information about most cabinet decisions. Even those who were in the cabinet room when specific decisions were taken (or as decisions were made elsewhere) often have very different perceptions of what transpired. And, of course, access to formal records or to central figures willing to speak frankly is severely limited. Similarly, it would be exceedingly difficult to systematically identify instances where first ministers or their staff meddled in the affairs of departments against the wishes or without the knowledge of the responsible ministers.

Yet though the criteria all but defy precise delineation and the fragmentary evidence tends to be either anecdotal or broadly impressionistic, this mug's game is worth playing. The topic of prime ministerial power is too important not to be confronted. Moreover, to admit from the outset that we can never hope for a definitive, all-times-all-places answer is not to say that we cannot substantially improve our understanding of the first minister's influence in cabinet and the core executive.

THE FIRST MINISTER AS BOSS: ASSESSING THE EVIDENCE

Without a shadow of doubt, the first minister is the boss: "the guy who breaks our nine to five ties," in an Ontario minister's telling phrase. Even a premier like British Columbia's Mike Harcourt, who believed strongly in governing by consensus (critics simply described him as weak), was nonetheless forthright about the exercise of his power: "Nineteen times out of twenty, cabinet and caucus work on the basis of genuine consensus, but there is also that one time that the premier's prerogative rules ... there were times that I just had to say 'this is the way it's going to be' ... in those instances, there were eighteen ministers but I had nineteen votes" (Harcourt 1996).

Many ministers and premiers interviewed mentioned some variation of this nineteen-vote rule. In Ontario under Bill Davis, a slightly different expression captured the dominant role of the premier: when the word came down that "the boss wants it," ministers understood that there was no point engaging in debate. As one of Gary Filmon's political advisors commented, "If the premier brings forward an agenda item, not too many people [ministers] will challenge it." A BC minister forthrightly acknowledged, "Nobody's going to cross him [the premier]; he's the boss ... you're only there by virtue of his choice."

Yet first ministers' power varies a good deal depending on a range of contextual factors. Certain policy sectors, such as foreign policy for the prime minister or constitutional negotiations for the premiers, are often accepted as falling primarily within the first minister's domain. Additionally, each first minister has a particular set of issues or policy fields on which he or she lavishes special attention and takes an unusually active role. Similarly, not all ministers are created equal: weak or inexperienced ministers are victimized by autocratic prime ministerial behaviour far more readily than tough, able, experienced ministers. As well, first ministers' capacity to impose their will on cabinet surely varies with political track records and career phases. Thus a premier who has successfully carried his party to electoral victory is in a stronger position vis-à-vis cabinet than one who has yet to face the electorate, having come to office through an internal party process.

Recognizing this variability in the exercise of first ministers' power helps make sense of apparently contradictory interpretations of a given prime minister: one minister or official's experience may be of a highly autocratic first minister while another may perceive the same person as acquiescing to ministerial preferences and accepting cabinet consensus.

This point is significant in that much of what we know, or think we know, of first ministerial autocracy comes from the accounts of ministers and senior bureaucrats. Some of Savoie's (1999) most compelling evidence takes the form of observations by current and former ministers and senior officials about the power structure within the core executive. Time and again he quotes central figures in the Chrétien and Mulroney governments decrying the concentration of power at the centre and highlighting the magnitude of change from the Pearson and even the Trudeau eras. Such evidence cuts both ways, though. For example, in a response to the Savoie thesis, Benoît Bouchard, a prominent Mulroney minister, agrees that the system "gave the Prime Minister, especially on important issues, almost absolute power." He adds, however, that while the plenary cabinet – some forty strong under

Mulroney – was usually too unwieldy to act as a true decision-making forum, ministers did exercise significant authority through the cabinet committee system and within their own departments. In his experience, although cabinet sometimes was a focus group for the prime minister, at other times it was very much a genuine decision-making body (Bouchard 1999, 2).

In assessing to what extent and under what circumstances Canadian first ministers can and do act autocratically to ignore or override their cabinets, it is also essential to recognize that a prime minister's public image may be an unreliable guide to his or her actual behaviour behind closed cabinet doors. As Bakvis suggests, "The more popular or media-centred depiction of the prime minister as an autocrat may be more of a caricature than an accurate portrait" (Bakvis 2001, 69). Both personal interviews with ministers and the limited writings of ministers and senior political and bureaucratic officials attest that first ministers widely perceived in the press and the public as domineering and autocratic were in reality far less dictatorial in cabinet and in their dealings with individual ministers than commonly thought.

Perhaps the figure whose public persona varied most dramatically from that described by his colleagues and officials is Prime Minister Trudeau. Widely perceived as arrogant and authoritarian in imposing his will within government, Trudeau emerges quite differently from the accounts of those who worked closely with him. Eugene Whelan, Trudeau's minister of agriculture, says quite simply, "Contrary to what many people think, Trudeau ran his Cabinet with a very loose hand ... I always laughed when people described him as a dictator" (Whelan 1986, 195). Mitchell Sharp, who served as a minister under both Pearson and Trudeau and who observed the St. Laurent cabinet first-hand as a senior bureaucrat, commented, "Trudeau was a remarkably effective chairman of cabinet – firm yet fair. I never knew him to anticipate a decision by giving his own opinion before asking the opinions of his colleagues, except, of course, with respect to constitutional questions. He genuinely sought for consensus. His reorganization of cabinet procedure illustrated his insistence upon orderly debate and his support for collegiality" (Sharp 1994, 167).

To be sure, Trudeau on occasion engaged in autocratic behaviour. Don Johnston, a senior minister, recalled his reaction to Trudeau's announcement that he had established a Royal Commission on the Economic Union and Development Prospects for Canada (the Macdonald Commission): "The Prime Minister's announcement struck me with the force of a lightning bolt. As Minister of State for Economic and Regional Development, it was inconceivable to me that such a Royal Commission would be named without proper consultation with the Minister of Finance, Marc Lalonde, and myself ... the Prime Minister had just told Canadians that a Royal Commission on the economy, which he judged would be of equal importance to the Rowell-Sirois Commission, had been named without consulting Cabinet" (Johnston 1986, 72).

Similarly, Jean Chrétien contemplated resigning as minister of finance over Trudeau's unilateral imposition – without so much as informing him – of sweeping spending reductions upon returning from an economic summit in Bonn (Chrétien 1985, 117). In his memoirs, Trudeau tacitly admitted that he should have involved Chrétien in the decision but argued that the decision was much less precipitous than it appeared: "Months before going to Bonn I had met with the Cabinet and told every minister that we had to cut spending to keep inflation in check. We had even prepared precise targets for every department to attain. But on my return from Bonn, I discovered that the ministers had offered up only 10 per cent of what we had requested ... sometimes you just have to move" (Trudeau 1993, 199). Chrétien himself referred to this episode as an uncharacteristic intervention, and described Trudeau's approach to cabinet as follows: "In cabinet Trudeau listened more and compromised more than most Canadians imagine ... I never subscribed to the notion that Trudeau was a dictator. Often knowing what he thought, I saw him accepting the views of his ministers despite his own wishes. He was extraordinarily patient, he let everyone have a say, and he listened attentively" (Chrétien 1985, 75).

Trudeau is by no means the only Canadian first minister who was popularly seen as riding roughshod over his cabinet but whom ministers and officials found neither domineering nor autocratic. For example,

Sterling Lyon of Manitoba and British Columbia's Bill Bennett, who cultivated a public image as a "tough guy" (Garr 1985), were widely thought to be dictatorial in cabinet. The clear consensus of the many ministers interviewed, however, was that these premiers paid close attention to the views of individual ministers and of cabinet collectively, only infrequently directly imposing decisions. Like Trudeau, they could be ruthless and uncompromising in dealing with political opponents, which doubtless accounts in part for the assumption that they acted similarly in cabinet.

One of Lyon's ministers noted that he "had a very high regard for cabinet as an institution" and consequently didn't impose his will on cabinet; because he didn't want ministers to proceed with policy without having cleared it through cabinet, he applied this principle to himself. Other ministers described Lyon's acceptance of cabinet decisions in very similar terms. A central agency bureaucrat closely involved with cabinet supported this view, maintaining that "Lyon was not nearly as dictatorial toward his ministers as his public image had it and often acceded to cabinet's views over his own." The following comments by (three different) Bennett ministers typify how he was perceived by those in and around his cabinet: "Bill Bennett was very good at consensus building; he didn't shove ideas down people's throats"; "[Bennett] generally accepted what cabinet had said; if faced with strenuous and widespread opposition, he didn't act unilaterally"; "he was quite open to discussion; he could be talked out of a bad idea ... Bill Bennett liked to seek the counsel of his ministers."

Now the ministers quoted in this chapter do not constitute anything like a representative sample of those who served in the cabinets that were closely studied for this project. Typically, the ministers interviewed were the most able and astute by virtue of their ability and experience; in other words, they were the strongest and most important. These were the ministers most likely to be included in the premier's inner circle and to be willing and able to stand up to him. Doubtless weaker or junior ministers might have portrayed premiers rather differently, but for our purposes the views and experiences of weak ministers are not as interesting or significant as those of strong ministers. It doesn't take an autocrat to push a weak minister around. And strong, successful first ministers typically have strong ministers in their cabinets.

The accounts of ministers and officials point to a crucial reason first ministers have their way with cabinet: with remarkable consistency, cabinet insiders emphasized that premiers were smarter, more experienced, harder working, and more clearly focused than anyone else around the cabinet table. Gordon Robertson wrote, for example, of "the methodical and penetrating scrutiny Trudeau directed at every cabinet document that came forward. He read every page and his superb mind detected any inconsistencies or problems" (Robertson 2000, 257). Provincially, the following comments are illustrative:

Manitoba bureaucrat: "Ed Schreyer dominated cabinet because he worked harder and was more disciplined than the other ministers."

Manitoba bureaucrat: "[Intellectually] Lyon stood head and shoulders above the rest of the cabinet."

Manitoba politico: Gary Filmon was able to dominate cabinet because "he knows so much [from his experience and contacts] ... ministers rarely bring more to the table than he already knows."

BC minister: Despite his lack of formal education, "Bill Bennett was by far the most rounded, well-informed person in cabinet."

Nova Scotia politico: John Buchanan was successful because "he was tougher – physically, mentally, and emotionally – than all the others."

Ontario minister: "Everyone respected his [Bob Rae's] judgment and intelligence and his political instincts ... no matter how well prepared you were on a submission, he was always two steps ahead of you, asking about implications down the road you hadn't even thought of."

Several cabinet office bureaucrats mentioned premiers who typically reviewed – often in minute detail – the entire cabinet book of submissions prior to meetings, whereas few ministers had the inclination or time to do so.

The first minister's edge in being in a position to carefully review all cabinet documents reflects a structural advantage inherent in the premiership. Without the pressures and day-to-day demands arising from portfolio responsibilities, the first minister may be the only one (save perhaps the finance minister) with the time and the analytic support to appraise thoroughly everything coming before cabinet. (Prime ministers and premiers often reserve for themselves the portfolio responsible for constitutional issues or federal-provincial relations, but these are typically extensions of their normal responsibilities.) Moreover, only the first minister has call on sufficient staff to provide expertise and advice on all manner of policy proposals. In practical terms, provincial premiers may be qualitatively better off than the prime minister in this regard. The range and scale of the issues arising before the federal cabinet, together with the colossal demands on the prime minister's time and attention, may mean that the advantages accruing to premiers from not having portfolio responsibilities are not realized in Ottawa.

Another inherent advantage enables first ministers to get their way without resorting to such crude exercises of power as vetoing a proposal with solid cabinet support or dictating a course of action to cabinet. First ministers control cabinet processes, from overall structural design – the mandate and composition of cabinet committees – to specific operational details such as setting the cabinet agenda and guiding the actual discussion. (While other ministers may chair cabinet meetings, it is crystal clear that first ministers are free to intervene in or terminate the discussion at any time.) Thus first ministers appoint trusted allies to chair key committees (or chair them themselves), decide the opportune time to place tricky items on the cabinet agenda, curtail debate on specific matters, send them back for further committee or bureaucratic review, or simply delay decisions. They also time their interventions for desired effect. Most first ministers typically hold back on presenting their views in cabinet until debate has unfolded, in order to benefit from their ministers' perspectives and advice. When on occasion they weigh in at the start of a discussion, they can significantly influence it. Control of the process thus gives the first minister a decided advantage. Whether this constitutes auto-cratic behaviour is a matter of definition; only first ministers have the prerogative of manipulating the decision-making process to achieve their goals, yet effective use of such privileges depends at least as much on astute, skilful management as on political muscle.

Former Ontario premier Bill Davis was said by one cabinet official to be masterful at "playing with the cabinet agenda" – delaying or revisiting items or bringing them forward at opportune moments – not only to defuse conflict but to ensure the outcomes he favoured without appearing heavy-handed. Such behaviour may have been manipulative, taking advantage of the first minister's privileged position, but at least it had an element of transparency for the ministers concerned, unlike BC premier Bill Bennett's practice, during his early years in office, of not sharing the cabinet agenda with his ministers. One minister spoke of knowing what was up for discussion at cabinet meetings only by walking near the premier and peeking over his shoulder at the agenda!

When the first minister makes tactical use of control over cabinet procedure, blocking a proposal is easier than realizing one. As former Manitoba premier Ed Schreyer put it in an interview, "Sometimes the best strategy is to hold off the decision until the tide of opinion changes ... the premier's position is much stronger on the negative side than on the positive; the premier cannot force something to proceed if there is no consensus in cabinet for it, but if the premier opposes a pro-posal he can exercise his authority to hold it back." And yet, the formi-dable strategic advantage of being able to manipulate the cabinet agenda has its limits: "Given the political challenge of finding Cabinet unity and the political strength of certain Cabinet ministers, there is a limit to how long a prime minister will want or will be able to keep a contentious issue off the agenda of Cabinet" (Thomas 2003-4, 82).

CASE STUDY: GLEN CLARK, THE ULTIMATE AUTOCRAT?

The exceptional case of former BC premier Glen Clark, who held power from 1996 to 1999, is instructive on the question of autocratic first ministers. No recent Canadian first minister has been accused, by outside observers and cabinet insiders alike, of such dictatorial practices as Clark. One long-time deputy minister explicitly described him as "autocratic," adding that few ministers were prepared to stand up to him. Prominent ministers spoke of Clark's micromanaging their departments, taking over files both crucial and trivial, and bypassing cabinet to place power in highly politicized central agencies. "The heads of the central agencies were the real decision makers," said one. "The rest of us [ministers] were told to toe the line." One veteran NDP political operative likened Clark to a traditional Scottish chieftain: as ruthless in maintaining his authority as vicious in fighting his enemies, every now and again killing one of his retinue to ensure fear and loyalty: "It was a gang: a little bit of terror to keep people in line and lots of rewards ... it's a good thing BC premiers don't control the military." Another, referring to the so-called triumvirate of powerful and strongly politicized central agency leaders around Clark, noted that the Clark premiership was marked by "testosterone politics – there were no girls allowed in the clubhouse – it was an exceedingly aggressive style," in which numerous and notorious violations of cabinet process reflected "a secretive and manipulative political culture emanating from the Premier's Office."

Even for the rough and tumble world of BC politics, these are remarkable comments from one's supposed political allies. Clark and his close advisors reject such extreme renderings of his premiership, while accepting that he consciously adopted a strong, "get the job done" style, very much centred on Clark. In his words,

> The premier can't impose his or her will on cabinet except in unusual and rare circumstances ... they're your colleagues and it is cabinet government; you have to respect their opinions ... cabinet was much more engaged when I was premier [than under his predecessor, Mike Harcourt]. I tried to ensure that cabinet meetings moved along better, were shorter and more decisive ... it was widely believed that I ran everything in government, but that was

preposterous – you can't run a government from the Premier's Office. I did try to master all the briefs and was pretty knowledgeable about a lot of things; this may have given people the impression that I was running everything.

I did dominate the discussion, but there was still much more discussion focused on the issues [than under Harcourt] because I made sure that there were clear choices before cabinet [and because] I forced ministers to take positions.

"Usually," recalled the former premier, "I would give my opinion characterizing the issue as I saw it at the beginning of the meeting; sometimes I would take over the presentation of the issue from the minister." Though in retrospect he realized that this may not have been a good idea, as it skewed the debate and emphasized his role over the minister's, he maintained that this was not equivalent to imposing his views on cabinet. On only one occasion, Clark said, did he explicitly overrule a clear majority of ministers, whereas he went along with cabinet majorities several times on important issues when he was convinced cabinet had it wrong.

Clark acknowledged that the circumstances of his accession to power initially required a one-man-band approach to decisions. He came to office after Mike Harcourt had resigned amid the "Bingogate" scandal, with the NDP seemingly headed for sure defeat in the looming election. Early on in his premiership, cabinet balked at Clark's plan on an electorally important issue; in his words, he told cabinet, "If we're going to pull this [the election] out, you're going to have to give me some running room." Cabinet accepted his terms, with the result that as the election approached and unfolded, "I made all kinds of commitments without cabinet approval or support." In consequence, "I had become so dominant [over cabinet], but you can't govern like that, though it took a while to reduce my dominance." This ascendancy was reinforced, Clark subsequently recognized, because "the media had gotten used to coming to me on anything government was doing." He revelled in – and excelled at – being the centre of media attention, but came to

94

realize that it would have been better to take a lower profile and refer the media to the responsible ministers.

According to Clark's advisors, he was a supremely activist premier who did not so much act autocratically toward cabinet as give it much-needed direction and energy. "Ministers," said one, "became overly cautious and deferential and resorted to the excuse 'I'd like to do this but the Premier's Office won't let me.'" One member of the "triumvirate" observed, "We failed because of inadequate centralization ... we had enough strength at the centre to bite off big chunks, but not enough to chew."

Clark's demurral on the charge of being dictatorial (and the comments of his close advisors) could be dismissed as the defensiveness of the guilty. Indeed it is hard to avoid the conclusion that Clark was an unusually autocratic first minister – his own statements warrant as much. Yet there was more to the Clark premiership than simply a power-hungry leader. Contextual factors loom large. Clark delivered what one of his ministers called "a miraculous electoral victory," returning the NDP to power in the face of certain defeat. Accordingly, cabinet and caucus felt an unusual sense of obligation to Clark. As well, the NDP's hold on power was tenuous at best, with a scant three-seat margin in the legislature – a situation calling for strong unity and cohesion, which Clark felt it his duty and right to impose. Some of Harcourt's stronger ministers had either been defeated in the election or were otherwise not in a position to challenge Clark. And even Clark's toughest critics acknowledge that he is fearsomely bright and politically astute. Doubtless Clark was autocratic, but to what extent was this a function of a confluence of highly unusual circumstances?

For all this, it is uncertain how long Glen Clark would have stayed at the helm even in the absence of live television coverage of a police raid on his house for evidence of bribery and corruption (charges of which he was subsequently cleared). Enormous pressure was building up within the NDP, both among party activists and MLAs and ministers, that might well have resulted in his ouster quite apart from the corruption scandal. His autocratic ways might well have brought about a cabinet revolt, resulting in his disposition.

The View from the First Minister's Chair

As the Clark situation illustrates, assessing the autocratic tendencies among Canadian first ministers is not an either/or proposition. Rather, it is a case of seeking to determine where the balance point lies between first ministers dictating to their cabinets and accepting their views. Probably every Canadian prime minister or premier has on occasion overruled a clear cabinet consensus on a major policy question or ignored cabinet altogether in proceeding with a particular course of action. Savoie cites several well-known incidents of prime ministers acting unilaterally without cabinet approval, including Trudeau's decision to slash expenditures on his return from the Bonn conference in 1978, Mulroney's massive bail-out for Saskatchewan farmers, and Chrétien's spur-of-the-moment spending commitments to various premiers (Savoie 1999, 75-6, 166).

Similar episodes dot provincial politics. Ontario premier Bill Davis reversed his government's long-standing policy on separate school funding, and purchased a large interest in an oil company. Bill Bennett decided to proceed with Expo '86. Bill Vander Zalm announced a stridently anti-abortion policy without consulting his cabinet, and imposed the Expo lands deal. Mike Harris secretly authorized a tax break for pro sports teams. If these unilateral actions occasioned ministerial grumbling, they were nonetheless generally accepted as legitimate exercises of the first minister's authority. Such episodes constitute powerful evidence for the first minister as autocrat thesis.

Significant as they may have been, however, they are nonetheless isolated and generally accepted as exceptional rather than typical. A true autocrat imposes his will on subordinates on a regular basis. Additionally, although instances of autocratic behaviour could be cited for all Canadian first ministers, it is similarly true that all manner of Canadian first ministers, from Ed Schreyer and John Buchanan to Bill Vander Zalm and Bob Rae, have emphasized the importance of persuading cabinet rather than dictating to it. They recognized the need to husband powers by occasionally giving in – both to individual ministers and to cabinet collectively – in order to be in a position to overrule cabinet or impose an outcome from time to time:

> [In "calling the consensus"] the premier has a great deal of discretionary authority, but in all cases does seek a genuine consensus of cabinet ... if I had too blatantly misstated the consensus, I would have been challenged (Ed Schreyer).

> Nobody expected to win all the time, not even the premier. A premier has a reserve power to make an opinion stick. But he or she is unwise to exercise that power except in very pressing circumstances (Allan Blakeney in Blakeney and Borins 1998, 31).

> Sometimes, as premier, you have to give in one circumstance in order to get in another (Bill Vander Zalm).

> The premier can't impose his or her will on cabinet except in unusual and rare circumstances ... they're your colleagues and it is cabinet government; you have to respect their opinion (Glen Clark).

> For the premier, getting things done is always an act of persuasion ... as premier, you're allowed a few issues on which cabinet understands that you feel strongly and that the boss is going to get his way, but there aren't very many of those; you just can't run a one-person government ... on the other hand, there were certainly times when I saw that a minister felt very strongly about something, and I might not have agreed, but I deferred to what the minister wanted to do (Bob Rae).

> I would sometimes give in on minor matters so I could come down heavy on the big issues (Howard Pawley).

> I didn't very often overrule the consensus of cabinet ... the premier can't be a dictator; that leads to [cabinet] disintegration (John Buchanan).

Former premiers might be suspected of downplaying their autocratic tendencies, but their ministers' recollections generally corroborate these accounts. Moreover, first ministers often went out of their way to elicit as broad a range of views from their ministers as possible. Glen Clark, for example, recounted that "I forced ministers to take positions on matters we were discussing; I'd go around the table and ask what people thought – maybe it would be only 'yes' or 'no' but ministers couldn't just sit there." David Peterson adopted an approach that "encouraged and rewarded people [ministers and bureaucrats] to disagree with me." Peterson prompted ministers and staff to challenge his views out of concern that "the premier is always the funniest guy in the room; the danger is that people are too deferential." Time and again, interviewed ministers (as well as the bureaucrats and politicos who frequented the cabinet room) remarked on premiers' willingness to listen attentively and prolong debate, to ensure that they were hearing the full spectrum of their ministers' views.

Admittedly, encouraging ministers to say their piece and listening intently is not at all equivalent to abiding by the democratic will of cabinet. Indeed, premiers and ministers alike acknowledge that, ultimately, first ministers need not follow the views of cabinet. Yet they also acknowledge the very real political constraints that impede the raw imposition of the first minister's will on cabinet. And first ministers taking seriously the views and advice of their cabinets as well as limiting the extent to which they ignore or overrule cabinet – in effect, husbanding their power – is inconsistent with the first minister as autocrat interpretation.

Moreover, strong ministers may not passively accept first ministers' attempts to intervene unduly in their portfolios but may well push back. Although on certain key issues, first ministers can be assured of getting their way, these are not everyday occurrences. An episode recounted by former Saskatchewan minister Janice MacKinnon illustrates the point. MacKinnon became aware that Premier Roy Romanow was holding meetings with top officials about a crucial issue in her department without including her. "In government," she writes, "if you don't stand your ground you soon find that there is no ground on which to stand. At a cabinet meeting where it was obvious that the premier was making decisions in my portfolio without my involvement, I spoke out ... I told him that if I was going to be the one who had to face the cameras and defend the decisions, I needed to be included in all the meetings ... I never again caught them meeting behind my back" (MacKinnon 2003, 88). Not all ministers possess the political moxie to confront the first minister openly in this fashion, nor would all such episodes end as happily for the minister – not only did Romanow accede to MacKinnon's demands, he subsequently promoted her to minister of finance – but doubtless more than a few do. Subservience breeds autocratic behaviour, whereas the typical strong, successful minister is not subservient but tough, aggressive, and not easily pushed around.

Cabinet is a multifunctional body. Though rendering decisions is certainly one of its principal roles, cabinet is also called upon to scan the political and policy environment for problems and opportunities, to monitor government performance, to develop overall plans and strategic directions, and to test ideas for policy suitability and political soundness. In performing these functions it is often helpful and appropriate for cabinet to act as a sounding board for the first minister. Otherwise put, an astute first minister does use cabinet as a focus group. To acknowledge this is by no means to dismiss the authority and influence of cabinet collectively or ministers individually when cabinet is engaged in decision making.

First Ministers: Powerful but Not Autocratic

What Patrick Weller has written of Australia doubtless applies to Canada: "The influence of the prime ministers and their impact on policy will depend on their capacity to cajole, persuade or bully cabinet colleagues – either individually or collectively – into accepting their approach or their solutions" (Weller 1992b, 5). Bullying, presumably the mark of an autocratic first minister, is only one possible strategy.

The argument of this chapter has been that while Canadian first ministers can and do override or ignore their cabinets on specific (sometimes crucial) decisions, the notion that they exercise supreme and unassailable power is overblown and runs contrary to the evidence. As Paul Thomas suggests, the first minister as autocrat argument rests on a key but overly simplistic assumption, "that power resides in one location and is finite in nature ... relationships within the political executive are seen as zero-sum games, in which there can be only winners and losers" (Thomas 2003-4, 80). The reality is rather more complex, reflecting fluid, interdependent power relationships in which "the Prime Minister needs on most occasions the uncoerced support of his ministers and to a lesser extent his backbench followers." Additionally, "The constitutional principle of individual ministerial responsibility and the tyranny of the clock oblige the prime minister to share authority and power with other Cabinet members. Most government activity today consists of running and modifying existing programs in their details – not matters that usually attract prime-ministerial attention" (85).

The remarkable contretemps between Prime Minister Chrétien and Paul Martin stands as a metaphor for the exercise of the first minister's power. The prime minister deployed his unquestioned power to dismiss Martin, despite his enormous popularity – quite possibly exceeding that of Chrétien himself – among the public, Liberal activists, and the Liberal caucus. And yet the reaction against Martin's firing so undermined the prime minister's position in the country, the party, and indeed in the parliamentary caucus that he found it necessary to announce his retirement lest he face the possibility of being forced from office.

Though this chapter has raised qualifications about and cast doubts on the more extreme versions of the prime minister as autocrat thesis, it has not challenged the basic argument put forward by Savoie, Simpson, and others: Canadian first ministers do wield remarkable power even by the standards of Westminster cabinet-parliamentary systems. Accordingly, although the more strident alarms about the threat to Canadian democracy represented by this concentration of power can be discounted, measures to curtail the power of first ministers would clearly enhance the quality of democracy in this country. Some possibilities are discussed in the concluding chapter.

Chapter 3

Strengths

- The extensive power wielded by Canadian first ministers is subject to important constraints.

- No first minister can govern single-handedly; successful first ministers rely on strong ministers, whose opinions they must take seriously.

- The Canadian first minister is "the boss," capable of imposing his or her will on any given issue or decision. Despite occasional instances of autocratic behaviour, Canadian first ministers cannot and do not routinely act autocratically.

Weaknesses

- Significant evidence supports the claim that the already formidable concentration of power enjoyed by the prime minister and the political-bureaucratic apparatus surrounding him or her has been growing largely unchecked.

- Provincial government is premiers' government: within their own systems, provincial premiers are more powerful than the prime minister is at the national level.

- Canadian first ministers are more powerful than their counterparts in Australia, Ireland, New Zealand, and the United Kingdom.

- The Canadian practice of selecting and removing party leaders by vote of party members, while democratic in certain ways, has significantly enhanced the power of the first minister.

4

PUBLIC PARTICIPATION
IN CABINET PROCESSES?

In June 1985, after forty-two consecutive years of Tory rule, David Peterson's Liberal Party took power in Ontario. Stressing a new openness and inclusiveness, Peterson promised a government "without walls or barriers" to the ebullient crowd watching his cabinet being sworn in on the lawn of the Legislative Building. As journalist Rosemary Speirs recounts, however, open government extended only so far:

> During cabinet the next day, Peterson noticed a middle-aged woman whom he didn't know. There were lots of new faces around these days, however ... Peterson leaned back in his chair between treasurer Robert Nixon and education minister Sean Conway and inquired quietly behind his hand just who the woman was. Conway replied that she was probably with the cabinet office. So Peterson signalled [Cabinet Secretary] Ed Stewart and asked him to make the introduction. "I thought she was with you," Stewart said in surprise. He then asked her business and was told: "I came to see the open government." She was politely, but firmly, ushered out (Speirs 1986, 184).

This story is amusing precisely because public observation of — let alone public participation in — cabinet processes is inherently unthinkable. And yet, in certain limited ways, Canadian cabinets have been willing to leave the door to the cabinet room ever so slightly ajar. Full cabinet and cabinet committees may engage in tours and public meetings outside the capital, they may hold closed cabinet meetings at which representatives of organized interest groups present briefs or hold discussions with ministers, and, *mirabile dictu,* in British Columbia some cabinet meetings are televised and cabinet agendas and submissions are posted on the Internet. In some jurisdictions, government backbenchers attend and participate in meetings of full cabinet or of cabinet committees. Additionally, the government caucus may, with varying degrees of formality and influence, advise on or vet cabinet decisions.

This chapter examines public access to and participation in cabinet processes through these possibilities. It also looks at the extent to which the public has access to cabinet documents and whether the opportunity to petition cabinet against decisions of semi-independent agencies constitutes a significant democratic inroad.

Deputations to Cabinet

As a rule, neither individuals nor organized groups can expect to participate in cabinet meetings. Exceptions occur, but under what circumstances? Who is invited into the cabinet room? Cabinet officials were asked whether "outside" groups and individuals, defined as persons other than political staff and public servants (including staff of government agencies), ever appeared before cabinet or its committees. (As discussed in Chapter 5, small numbers of senior public servants and partisan advisors regularly attend cabinet, but they are in no way "the public.") As well, they were asked whether the impetus for such meetings lay with cabinet or with the outside groups, and about confidentiality provisions. The results are summarized in Tables 4.1 and 4.2. These data do not include tours and meetings outside the capital, or the numerous meetings of individual ministers with stakeholders, interest groups, or outside advisors.

Care is required in specifying just what appearing before cabinet entails. It is rare in the extreme for outside organizations or individuals to observe or participate in formally constituted cabinet meetings and rarer still for them to be in the room when cabinet decides an issue. Groups or individuals may well meet with the entire cabinet, often in the cabinet room, but not while the cabinet is in formal session. Otherwise put, when delegations come before cabinet or cabinet committees, they typically do so to consult with or provide information and advice to cabinet rather than to participate in decision making. Since what is at issue is the opportunity to address cabinet and exchange views with it, both formal and informal meetings are included in the following discussion.

As Tables 4.1 and 4.2 demonstrate, most Canadian jurisdictions permit groups or individuals to appear before cabinet or cabinet committee, though save in Alberta, where as many as 100 groups a year meet with cabinet committees, these are not frequent occurrences. The upper limit for full cabinet is about a half-dozen meetings a year, reached in Prince Edward Island, Manitoba, and Saskatchewan (see Table 4.1). In Saskatchewan the number was, until recently, significantly higher. Under Premier Roy Romanow, who held office from 1991 to 2001, "the practice was to set aside four days a year and schedule organizations who had submitted requests for one hour presentations – average was about six per day." His successor, Lorne Calvert, decided "to deal with requests as they were received and some were scheduled for meetings with full cabinet and some were handled by smaller groups of specific ministers" (Saskatchewan Executive Council Office, response to questionnaire, 2002). Instances of cabinet committees meeting with outside groups are not much more numerous, again with the exception of Alberta (see Table 4.2).

The change in Saskatchewan exemplifies an important characteristic of cabinet meetings with groups and individuals: cabinet's openness to such meetings waxes and wanes, and the first minister's preference is decisive. Similarly, in Ontario before 1995, under Conservative,

Table 4.1

Appearance of "outside organizations/individuals" before cabinet, 2002

Jurisdiction	Appear	Annual frequency	Origin of requests	Meetings in public	Meetings treated as confidential
Newfoundland and Labrador	Yes	1-2	Mostly from outside	No	Yes, "implicit expectation"
Prince Edward Island	Yes	4-6	75-80% from outside	No	Yes, but no formal requirement
Nova Scotia	No	—	—	—	—
New Brunswick	No	—	—	—	—
Quebec	No	—	—	—	—
Ontario	No	—	—	—	—
Manitoba	Yes	4-6	50% from outside	No	No[4]
Saskatchewan	Yes	7 in 2001	All from outside	No	No
Alberta	No	—	—	—	—
British Columbia	Yes[1]		All from cabinet	Yes, open cabinet No, others	No, open cabinet Yes, others
Yukon	Yes	2-3	50% from outside	No	Yes, though no formal process
Northwest Territories	Yes[2]	1-2	50% from outside	No	Yes, in cabinet No, with ministers
Nunavut	Yes[3]	—	50% from outside	No	Yes, in cabinet No, with ministers
Canada	No	—	—	—	—

1 CEOs of Crown corporations appear once a year, and a small number of others at "open cabinet."
2 At ministers' request, consultants working for government report at formal cabinet meetings but are not present for discussion of decision. Other requests are refused, though groups may meet with groups of ministers (perhaps all ministers) outside cabinet setting.
3 Formal policy is that "if there is a wish by members to discuss issues with persons [other than government officials] Cabinet will adjourn and a briefing session will be held for members of Cabinet."
4 Media sometimes attend.
Source: Responses to author's questionnaire, 2002.

Liberal, and NDP premiers, the cabinet met from time to time with broad umbrella organizations, but the Harris Conservative government did not accept delegations to cabinet.

Who are the fortunate few with access to cabinet? Generally they are representatives of organized interests, such as the Dairy Association of Newfoundland and Labrador, the University of Prince Edward Island Atlantic Veterinary College, and the Saskatchewan Mining Association. Less frequently, advisors or consultants come before cabinet to brief

Public Participation in Cabinet Processes?

Table 4.2

Appearance of "outside organization/individuals" before cabinet committees, 2002

Jurisdiction	Appear	Annual frequency	Origin of requests	Meetings in public	Meetings treated as confidential
Newfoundland and Labrador	Yes	1-2	Mostly from outside	No	Yes, "implicit expectation"
Prince Edward Island	Yes	1	Mixed	No	Yes, but no formal requirement
Nova Scotia	No	—	—	—	—
New Brunswick	Yes	1-2	All from outside	No	Yes
Quebec	No	—	—	—	—
Ontario	No	—	—	—	—
Manitoba	Yes	6-10	Mixed	Occasionally	No
Saskatchewan	No	—	—	—	—
Alberta	Yes	90-100	95% in public	75% in public	Yes, if meeting privately No, if in public
British Columbia	Yes	Monthly	90% from outside	Only rarely	No
Yukon	Yes	1-2	All from cabinet committee	No	Yes
Northwest Territories	Yes	2-3	All from ministers	No	Yes
Nunavut	No cabinet committees	—	—	—	—
Canada	Yes	Not available	All from cabinet committee	No	Not available

Source: Responses to author's questionnaire, 2002.

ministers on public policy issues; for example, the Yukon cabinet hears presentations from consultants hired to review certain policy questions, and the Newfoundland and Labrador cabinet met with an academic economist regarding a government initiative. The great bulk of cabinet and cabinet committee meetings with representatives of outside groups are in response to requests from such groups, though the initiative occasionally comes from the government side (in Ottawa, this is always the case). Most jurisdictions have no formal policy on meeting requests and deal with them on a case-by-case basis.

Public Participation in Cabinet Processes?

About three-quarters of the meetings with Alberta's cabinet committees occur in public, as does the occasional group appearance before British Columbia's "open cabinet"; otherwise these appearances are not public events. Cabinet confidentiality is obviously not an issue when meetings are public, but for the most part an expectation prevails that deputants will respect the confidentiality of discussions in the cabinet room. Those who meet with cabinet are not asked to sign confidentiality agreements or swear oaths; rather, meetings are presumed to be private affairs, like most meetings with individual ministers or senior bureaucrats. Saskatchewan is an exception here: "Meetings are often followed by media scrums which give the organizations an opportunity to report to the public on the issues raised with Cabinet" (Saskatchewan Executive Council Office, response to questionnaire, 2002). In Newfoundland and Labrador, the government routinely issues press releases citing ministers' commitment to address the issues raised by groups and quoting group leaders who pronounce themselves "pleased with the opportunity to meet with the [cabinet] committee" (Government of Newfoundland and Labrador 2001).

The occasional invitation to leaders of well-heeled, professional interest groups to meet privately with cabinet or its committees can only in the most limited sense be construed as *public* access to cabinet. These meetings may be useful for interest groups, though most reports suggest that they are too genteel and formal to constitute a particularly effective forum for lobbying. More progress is usually made through meetings with the individual ministers responsible for particular policy sectors. Significantly, when asked, many ministers commented that they usually found interest group deputations in cabinet or cabinet committees a waste of time. Overall, the occasional appearance of chambers of commerce, labour federations, medical associations, university presidents, and representatives of similar prominent organizations before cabinet represents at best a marginal advance for democracy.

Cabinet Travel

While ministers lacked enthusiasm for deputations to cabinet, they were much more positive about cabinet or committee tours that took them out of the capital. Canadian cabinets regularly meet outside the capital for two- or three-day retreats (sometimes accompanied by some or all government backbenchers) to develop long-term policy plans and political strategy. Typically, the schedule includes a media event or two and possibly a social gathering with local party faithful or community leaders. These retreats may have their uses for cabinet priority setting and group dynamics, but they are not, except in the most pro forma way, opportunities for public access.

Still, provincial cabinets have been known to travel en masse through the hinterlands beyond the capital. A BC minister of the Bill Bennett era spoke enthusiastically of the educational and political benefits cabinet gained from its annual forays (sometimes lasting a week or more) beyond Victoria and Vancouver, stopping in many communities to hear delegations, hold luncheons with local notables, visit ministry field offices, and so on. Though it is uncommon for full cabinet to engage in such extensive travel outside the capital, cabinets (and much less often, cabinet committees) do occasionally venture out to meet local leaders and interest group representatives or to hear from the public on specific issues.

Such travel is largely a provincial and territorial phenomenon, and is quite unusual at the federal level. The most prominent case of the federal cabinet engaging in such activities within recent memory was the Cabinet Committee on Canadian Unity, established in the aftermath of the Meech Lake Accord's demise. Though this committee held well-publicized meetings in locations across the country, these were not public meetings, nor were groups or individuals invited before it: "It was only during luncheon sessions or receptions at the out-of-town meetings that groups might have an opportunity to interact with individual ministers, but these sessions were not well advertised and invitations were available mainly through local Conservative MPs" (Bakvis and Hryciuk 1993, 130).

Genuine exercises in public consultation, sometimes with a definite policy focus, sometimes aimed at tapping into opinion beyond the immediate parliamentary precincts in an open-ended manner, seem to have become less common. When cabinet or cabinet committees tour they do so more as part of a communications campaign than in an authentic attempt at gathering information, ideas, and opinions. These developments are not surprising for several reasons. First, ministers are simply busier than their predecessors were two or three decades ago and thus less inclined to devote time to activities such as cabinet committee tours. Second, advances in communications technology, increasing sophistication on the part of interest groups, greater reliance on public opinion polling and focus groups, and similar developments have greatly expanded the range and quantity of information and advice available to ministers, thereby lessening the value they might see in leaving their offices to consult the public. Third, heightened media attention to ministerial behaviour – some might say the triumph of "gotcha journalism" – has raised the political stakes for ministers, especially groups of ministers, who take the unusual step of meeting formally with the public.

Although it pertains to community visits by the premier rather than by cabinet, the experience of Saskatchewan premier Allan Blakeney is germane here. During his 1971-82 premiership, Blakeney regularly toured the province in the "Blakeney Bus," meeting local residents informally, listening to their concerns, and discussing politics and policy with them. Initially, he found these gatherings politically useful opportunities to gauge public opinion. "As time went on," he recounts,

> either by accident or by design, people would come forward to raise issues in a belligerent way, and the press would report this in full colour. My staff then became more protective, and events became gradually more structured ... when fifty friendly contacts and one belligerent one produced a headline "PREMIER HAMMERED ON BUS TOUR," it was not clear what the best thing was for us to do. The tours almost imperceptibly became more media events instead of opportunities for me to meet in a relaxed way

with a cross-section of small-town Saskatchewan (in Blakeney
and Borins 1998, 63).

In order to move beyond anecdotes and accounts of individual premiers and their cabinets, let us consider the data in Table 4.3. This
table summarizes information provided by cabinet officials on cabinet
meetings and tours outside the capital. A similar table had been
planned on meetings and tours by cabinet committees; however, the
nearly universal aversion to travel by cabinet committees rendered it
pointless. Three provinces (Quebec, Alberta, and British Columbia)
reported rare instances of cabinet committees' meeting or touring outside the capital; in most jurisdictions it is unknown. Only in Newfoundland and Labrador do cabinet committees regularly venture around the
province to hold public and private meetings. Standing committees of
cabinet there hold as many as half a dozen meetings or tours a year
outside St. Johns, while ad hoc committees have been known to meet as
many as twenty times in various locations across the province. A
recent example is the round of "working visits" in 2001-2 by the Social
Policy of Cabinet to six regional centres to meet local committees
involved with the government's Strategic Social Plan.

All provincial and territorial cabinets routinely, if infrequently, hold
meetings outside the capital, as shown in Table 4.3. (The federal cabinet occasionally holds day-long retreats in places like Meech Lake, but
these venues are within the National Capital Region.) The Quebec and
Ontario cabinets venture out into their provinces only for retreats; they
neither hold regular meetings nor conduct tours, though when the
Ontario cabinet travels, public events are included on its itinerary. (In
his 2003 election manifesto, "The Road Ahead," Ontario premier Eves
promised regular cabinet visits throughout the province.) Cabinets in
all other provinces and territories typically meet outside their capitals
two or three times a year, though as many as six to ten times annually
in Prince Edward Island, Saskatchewan, Manitoba, and New Brunswick.

A single trip by cabinet could include a retreat, regular meetings,
and a tour (visits to several locations, often including meetings with
local officials and inspection of facilities or institutions). These three

Table 4.3

Cabinet travel, 2002

Jurisdiction	Annual frequency	Activities during trip			Other included activities		
		Retreats	Regular meetings	Tours	Public events	Meetings with local leaders	Individual minister meetings
Newfoundland and Labrador	1-2	1	1	—	No	Sometimes	Yes
Prince Edward Island	7-10	1 per year	All	Most	No	Yes	No
Nova Scotia	4	1	3	—	No	Yes	Yes
New Brunswick	6-9	1	5-8	—	Yes	Yes	Yes
Quebec	2	All	—	—	No	No	No
Ontario	0-1	All	—	—	Yes	Yes	Yes
Manitoba	6-8	—	All	—	Yes	Yes	Yes
Saskatchewan	About 6	1 per year	All but one	All but one	Yes	Yes	Yes
Alberta	1-3	1	1-2	—	Yes	Yes	Yes
British Columbia	2	1-2	1	1	Yes	Yes	Yes
Yukon	1-2	—	All	All	Yes	Yes	Yes
Northwest Territories	1	All	All	—	Yes	Yes	Yes
Nunavut	5-9	1-3	4-6	—	Yes	Yes	Yes
Canada	None	—	—	—	—	—	—

Source: Responses to author's questionnaire, 2002.

activities represent different possibilities for public access. Significantly, tours, which offer the best prospects for public access, are the least common; only four jurisdictions (PEI, Saskatchewan, British Columbia, and Yukon) reported that their cabinets engage in tours. Cabinet sallies beyond the usual confines of the capital normally also make provision for public events, for meetings with local community, economic, and political leaders, and for groups to meet privately with individual ministers. Such points of access are limited in time and scope and are doubtless subject to careful control and management by government and political officials. Circumscribed as they may be, however, they can represent valuable opportunities for interaction with cabinet by groups and individuals in regions not normally favoured with cabinet access – certainly far more than is possible when cabinet meetings take place in forbidding government buildings in distant capital cities well beyond public purview and without a hint of public access.

A similar conclusion emerges when the political purpose of cabinet travel is examined. Anyone who imagines that cabinet meetings outside the capital, other than the most hermetically sealed retreats, are anything other than highly political efforts at defending and promoting the government is naïve in the extreme. The record of the Liberal government in the Yukon (2000-2) is a telling example. Every few months the Yukon cabinet would head off for a two- or three-day tour of communities such as Ross River, Faro, Haines Junction, and Dawson; in addition to holding routine cabinet meetings, public events were scheduled, with Premier Pat Duncan encouraging her ministers to meet with as many groups and individuals as possible. The not-so-hidden agenda was to demonstrate to the voters that Duncan's Liberals were responsive to the entire territory and not just a "Whitehorse government" (a frequent criticism, since the Liberals held no seats outside the capital).

A similar calculus explains why one of the first acts of Prime Minister Martin's minority government following the July 2004 election was the organization of a two-day cabinet meeting in Kelowna, British Columbia. The strategic importance of BC voters for Liberal political fortunes clearly underlay what was only the Liberals' second cabinet meeting outside Ottawa since 1993. (The Kelowna meeting is not reflected in Table 4.3 since the tables in this chapter were constructed on the basis of data for 2002 and early 2003. Doubtless some entries were subsequently rendered inaccurate by changes in government – as in Ontario – or other factors, but the tables provide a snapshot of a particular point in time, demonstrating the variations and patterns across jurisdictions.)

While cabinet travel, and the public access associated with it, is ultimately an exercise in advancing the government's political interests, this by no means negates the value of that access. What matters is that groups and individuals, especially those far removed from the seat of power, have some measure of access to cabinet. The limited capacity for public participation in cabinet processes through cabinet tours and meetings outside the capital, however, is further circumscribed by the highly variable and impermanent nature of these opportunities. That is, lack of institutionalization is a significant impediment to the democratic potential of cabinet travel. Accordingly, it is worth briefly examining Australia, where such processes have become commonplace at the state level.

In the Australian states, cabinets have taken to regularly visiting remote communities, holding what are variously called "community cabinets," "regional cabinets," or "community forums." The slick newsletters and media statements on community cabinets found on government websites show these events have important public relations and political uses. For instance, the premier and various ministers often make regionally important announcements at these meetings. At the same time, they represent genuine opportunities for citizen access to cabinet. A Queensland bureaucrat offers the following account of community cabinet:

> Every three weeks cabinet is held over two days (Sunday-Monday) in regional communities ... A group of 100 people (ministers, ministerial advisors, departmental CEOs, premier's staff, and cabinet secretary) travel to selected communities – some of them very remote – and literally sit down on Sunday afternoon in a big sports venue or whatever big, open building is available, and talk to whoever wants to talk to them, about whatever they want to talk about. I refer to it as kitchen table politics, because we arrange 18 big tables or trestles (whatever is available) at which a minister, the departmental CEO, and a ministerial advisor sit and talk with individuals or small groups for ten to fifteen minutes each ... this is a very informal process – "jeans and tee-shirts," no suits, ties or formal presentations. Literally, a cup of tea or coffee and a chat – there is the odd protest about a local issue, but after all, that is democracy at work ...

[One recent] Community Cabinet took us to Winton, population 1,616, 1,500 km northwest of Brisbane. Six hundred farmers had come to the meeting to protest new vegetation management legislation – many of them having driven six to eight hours to get there. As most of the farms are large but economically marginal, one family operations, most had left either a wife or husband to keep operations going while the other came to talk to the premier and cabinet. Neither side may have agreed with what the other said, but at least the opportunity was there, in an open and informal forum for each side to state their case and hear how things looked from the other side. In addition to the usual five hours on Sunday afternoon, the premier held a three-hour meeting that night to ensure that everyone had their say (personal communications 1999; 2000).

Two academics who analyzed community cabinets in one state observed, on the one hand, "lively interaction between representatives and citizens" and, on the other, "a perception that Community Cabinets allow citizens to 'get things off their chest' without delivering real participation and substantial consultation in the activities of Government" (Bishop and Chalmers 1999). A survey of participants found that the typical person attending a community cabinet session is forty-five to seventy-five years old and already active in community and political affairs, which suggests that the process is not genuinely widening the range of persons interacting with government. The analysts interpret the survey as pointing to problems not so much in the community cabinet concept as in its reach (Bishop and Chalmers 2002). Overall, they see the community cabinet process as a novel bridge between two often incompatible models of democracy, in which "the appeal and approach of populism is used to direct attention to the legitimate workings of the institutions of representative government" (Bishop and Chalmers 1999).

British Columbia's Open Cabinet

If only very limited opportunities exist for groups and individuals to meet with cabinet and only infrequently does cabinet bestir itself to travel outside the capital, the prospects for the general public to observe cabinet in action are vanishingly small. And yet, the Liberal government in British Columbia holds monthly open cabinet meetings that are – astonishingly to traditionalists – fully televised. Live television coverage of cabinet meetings is easily dismissed as a bizarre blend of political naïveté and cynical posturing (especially given its genesis in Canada's prime spawning ground for loopy politics). Perhaps only a party like the BC Liberal Party, wholly bereft of government experience, would be so foolish as to promise to conduct cabinet business before the all-seeing eye. Similarly, in implementing such an absurd commitment, the only possible course of action would seem to lie in puffery and artifice, which bear no relation to the realpolitik of cabinet government. Yet this innovation merits closer inspection and at least temporary suspension of disbelief. The significance of televising cabinet for enhancing democracy in the core executive may depend less on how genuinely the BC Liberals are committed to openness than on the momentum and the unforeseen consequences that the open cabinet experiment generates.

While in opposition, the BC Liberal Party developed a wide-ranging reform agenda featuring a series of measures to foster openness and accountability in government, including a promise to televise cabinet meetings. Leader Gordon Campbell declared, "Trust and confidence [in government] start with transparency; we want to lift the veil on cabinet secrecy forever by holding full cabinet meetings at least once a month in public," promising that major issues would be "decided in public, not behind closed doors" (quoted in Palmer 2003a). On attaining office in the summer of 2001, the Liberals indeed opened one cabinet meeting a month to the public, with complete television coverage through the provincial parliamentary channel and the Internet. Additionally, transcripts of meetings, together with cabinet submissions, copies of slide presentations, and summaries of orders in council are posted on the government website (as are the detailed letters of instruction from the premier to his new ministers).

The first public cabinet meeting proved anodyne, featuring "zero debate and not much discussion" (Palmer 2001). And even at the start of this first meeting, a quarter of the twenty seats reserved for the public were empty (meetings are open to the public but do not include public participation). Several newsworthy announcements were made, generating substantial media interest. Subsequent meetings, some of which have taken place in regional centres such as Kelowna and Penticton, have been scarcely more authentic exercises in cabinet decision making. Typically, selected ministers make long, carefully scripted announcements and receive congratulatory comments and supportive questions from their colleagues; when it comes time for a "decision," the result is a foregone conclusion. Conflict, discord, and competition for resources or priority are notably absent (as are overt references to the political consequences of proposed policies). On occasion a ministerial presentation may generate a modicum of give and take between ministers. But while questions can be substantive and genuine, they uniformly seek clarification or explanation; they do not challenge ministers or their policies. Veteran journalist Vaughan Palmer's account of a recent open cabinet meeting noted that ministers not making presentations "posed some perfunctory questioning ... the better not to look bored. But no bona fide debates occurred and no decisions were made" (Palmer 2003a). At another meeting, a minor expression by the premier of annoyance at a minister proved a sufficient aberration from the normal run of rehearsed speeches to warrant media attention (Palmer 2003b).

If open cabinet has thus far clearly been a charade bearing almost no relation to real cabinet processes, why not dismiss it as just another west coast curiosity, offering no real public access to cabinet? While this judgment will probably be borne out, other outcomes could be imagined. For example, busy ministers may grow restless regularly devoting valuable time to a hollow public relations exercise, with the result that real debate, encompassing opposing points of view, will break out. Or Premier Campbell's background in municipal politics – where councils do reach important decisions in public – may overcome qualms about showing cabinet genuinely considering the pros and cons of proposed policies and ministers expressing differences of opinion, though the longer open cabinet proceeds in its current sham form, the less likely this seems.

No one seriously imagined that the public would be able to tune in to watch the cabinet thrash out important decisions. It remains to be seen whether British Columbia's open cabinet descends into total irrelevance or develops into something offering some slight public insight into the work of cabinet. Perhaps more important, and still unclear, is whether the open cabinet experiment advances or discredits ideas for unconventional cabinet structures and processes.

Backbench Participation in Cabinet Processes

Government backbenchers are hardly "the public"; any involvement they may have in the workings of cabinet cannot be construed as public participation in cabinet processes. They are, however, the public's representatives. Given the concentration of power in cabinet and its exclusionary nature, any indication that backbenchers, with their direct links to the public, are included in cabinet deliberations is worth pursuing. Let us look at the presence and participation of backbenchers in meetings of cabinet itself and in meetings of cabinet committees, as well as the role of the government caucus in vetting or approving cabinet decisions.

GOVERNMENT BACKBENCHERS AT CABINET AND CABINET COMMITTEE

As a preliminary, it should be emphasized that only members of the government caucus – that is, members elected by the party forming the government – have any possibility of participating in cabinet processes. MPs and MLAs from opposition parties need not apply. At that, as Table 4.4 shows, in many Canadian jurisdictions even government members have no better access to the cabinet room than those in opposition. Government backbenchers typically enjoy better access to individual ministers than do their opposition colleagues; their letters and calls are answered more quickly and fulsomely and their requests are likely to receive more favourable hearing. Yet being better placed to lobby and importune individual ministers (most commonly on constituency matters) is not the same as participating in cabinet processes on significant policy questions.

The table shows that government backbenchers in most of Canada do not attend, let alone participate in, meetings of full cabinet. East of Regina the frequency of government members attending cabinet ranged from "almost never" to "never." In some places, such as Quebec and Alberta, the chief government whip attends cabinet even if he or she does not hold ministerial rank. Elsewhere, for example in New Brunswick, the whip is not invited to cabinet; until recently the Saskatchewan whip attended cabinet meetings but only when House business was being discussed. Although the whip is no ordinary backbencher, this practice can represent an important modification to the general conclusion. Given that the whip is responsible not only for imposing discipline on private members but also for conveying backbench opinion to the party leadership, having the whip attend cabinet offers the possibility of improved cabinet-caucus liaison. This was precisely the rationale cited for the inclusion in the Martin cabinet of the chief government whip, in direct contrast to Prime Minister Chrétien's practice (Privy Council Office 2004).

Leaving the aside the special case of the whip, in the three Western provinces marked deviations from the prevailing pattern of backbench exclusion from cabinet meetings emerge. In Saskatchewan, two members of the government caucus attend meetings of cabinet. Backbenchers (including the whip) rotate through the two spots in month-long stretches, so that with a government caucus numbering barely over a dozen, the typical backbencher has two stints a year sitting in

Table 4.4

Backbench participation in cabinet and cabinet committees, 2002

Jurisdiction	Backbenchers attend cabinet?	Backbenchers have access to cabinet documents?	Backbenchers attend cabinet committees?	Backbenchers have access to cabinet committee documents?
Newfoundland and Labrador	Never/almost never	—	Yes, parliamentary secretaries regularly	Yes
Prince Edward Island	Never	—	Backbenchers are members of cabinet committees	—
Nova Scotia	Never/almost never	—	Never/almost never	—
New Brunswick	Never/almost never	—	Occasionally	No
Quebec	Never, except Whip	Yes	Rarely	—
Ontario	Never	—	Parliamentary assistants sit on some committees	Yes
Manitoba	Never/almost never	—	Never/almost never	—
Saskatchewan	Always	Yes	Yes, on Legislative Instruments Committee	Yes
Alberta	Always	Yes	Always	Yes
British Columbia	Monthly	Yes	Backbenchers are on all cabinet committees but one	Yes
Yukon	Occasionally	Yes	Never	—
Northwest Territories	Never	—	Never	—
Nunavut	Never/almost never	—	Never/almost never	—
Canada	Never/almost never	—	Never/almost never	—

Source: Responses to author's questionnaire, 2002.

on cabinet meetings. These MLAs do not receive cabinet documents in advance of the meeting, but are given them on entering the cabinet room and must return them to officials afterwards. In Alberta, in addition to the whip (who is not a minister) two members of the government caucus attend all meetings of full cabinet. These "caucus liaison" MLAs, one for the province's north and one for the south, are chosen by the premier and have full voting rights as well as full access to cabinet documents. In addition, the chairs of the standing policy committees (discussed below), who are backbenchers, participate in cabinet meetings when reports from their committees are considered. The practice in British Columbia has been less open: chairs of the hybrid cabinet-caucus committees (also discussed below) attend cabinet meetings on a monthly basis to report the results of committee review of legislation and policy submissions.

Several jurisdictions that do not permit government backbenchers to attend cabinet meetings are less restrictive when it comes to cabinet committees, as may be seen in Table 4.4. In Nova Scotia, New Brunswick, Quebec, and Ottawa, private government members are always or virtually always excluded from cabinet committees, but in other jurisdictions, backbenchers (usually parliamentary secretaries or assistants) routinely serve as members of or take part in cabinet committee meetings. Even in the more restrictive jurisdictions, exceptions occur, as in Nova Scotia, where caucus members were added to cabinet committees carrying out an extensive program review exercise in 1999-2000.

In Alberta cabinet committees per se do not exist. Instead, a series of caucus committees, styled standing policy committees, comprise both ministers and government backbenchers. The Agenda and Priorities Committee and Treasury Board, the two central and most powerful committees (chaired by the premier and the minister of finance, respectively), each consist of seven ministers and three backbenchers. When it comes to the half-dozen sectoral policy committees (such as Agriculture and Community Affairs or Economic Development and Finance), however, not only do private members serve as chairs, they outnumber ministers: each committee has three to five ministers (plus the premier, ex officio) and seven to nine private government members.

Recourse to caucus rather than cabinet committees can be traced to the 1970s, when Premier Peter Lougheed found himself with staggeringly lopsided majorities in the legislature (the 1979 election, for example, returned seventy-five Conservative and four opposition MLAs). This not only rendered conventional legislative committees impractical, but also raised the question of how to harness the energy and abilities of hordes of backbenchers or, more pragmatically, how to keep them busy and out of trouble. Lougheed established a series of sectoral caucus committees roughly parallel to cabinet committees, with a mandate to review government policies, question ministers, receive delegations, and less often, develop responses to specific political issues. Significant as these committees were, they were essentially reactive. Moreover, they were not formally integrated into the cabinet decision-making process, which featured a system of traditional cabinet committees from which backbenchers were excluded (McCormick 1983).

The current structure goes well beyond Lougheed's reform to involve private members directly in cabinet processes. In 1993 Premier Ralph Klein replaced all cabinet and caucus committees with standing policy committees, on most of which backbenchers outnumbered ministers, usually by only a small margin (10:8 on the Natural Resources and Sustainable Development Committee). Klein's stated objective was to "bring together Ministers and Private Members in a team-building approach to the development of public policy and afford the public more meaningful access to the government decision-making process" (Alberta 1993) – the latter in part a reference to the committees' mandate to hear submissions from nongovernmental delegations in public. The roster of committees has since expanded and contracted and the ratio of backbenchers to ministers has shifted as well, but the fundamental principle of backbencher participation in decision making remains. By 1998, an official account of the Alberta decision-making process noted "the 'Cabinet committee' distinction is simply not made anymore in Alberta" (Privy Council Office 1998, 107).

Do Alberta private members really enjoy the clout that their numerical preponderance and official government pronouncements suggest? Issues don't necessarily divide along minister-backbencher lines, and moreover, ministers sponsoring items under discussion carry substantial weight with their committee colleagues. But according to nonpartisan bureaucrats, these committees are marked by genuine equality of participation. Decisions are reached by formal vote, so that government backbenchers are in a position to overrule ministers on the committees. Committee recommendations may be revisited in full cabinet, though they are only reopened and reversed for good reason. According to officials in the Alberta Executive Council Office, the standing policy committees "were designed to be very flexible and to empower caucus, a goal the government believes it has achieved" (Privy Council Office 1998, 107). A skeptic might wonder if there are not ministers-only committees where the real decisions are taken. Alberta does indeed have such entities, called "ministerial task forces," but they are ad hoc in nature (on topics such as public sector bargaining and post-9/11 security) and do not have decision-making authority. Their work feeds into the policy process by way of the standing policy committees.

The skeptic might also object that this idyllic image of strong backbench involvement in cabinet processes seems at odds with what is widely seen as Alberta's "premier-centred" politics, of which Ralph Klein is a prime exemplar (Brownsey forthcoming; Martin 2002). One interpretation has it that government backbenchers do indeed play a strong and effective role in the standing policy committees, but that the real power in government rests elsewhere, primarily with a de facto inner cabinet – the Agenda and Priorities Committee – dominated by the premier. Indeed, in this account, what is significant in the Alberta cabinet decision-making process is not backbench influence through the hybrid committees but the centralization of power in the premier and the concomitant weakness of ministers, whether acting as individuals or in groups such as the policy committees. The structures may be unconventional, but they reinforce the province's traditional premier-dominated style, allowing "Klein to control all aspects of governance in the province. As a result, the premier frequently contradicts public statements of ministers and makes decisions with little or no formal consultation with cabinet" (Brownsey forthcoming). Whatever the real-life constraints on participation and influence by Alberta government backbenchers, however, their position vis-à-vis cabinet unquestionably carries more force than elsewhere in Canada.

Clearly the premier's predilections – most notably his willingness to involve private members in cabinet processes – have been central to the creation and operation of Alberta's cabinet-caucus committees. Lougheed was prepared to give caucus committees serious work to do, though as a "command and control" premier, he did not turn significant decision-making authority over to them. By contrast, Klein is said by bureaucrats to have a strong populist commitment to real caucus participation in decision making, reflecting his personal belief in the importance of MLA involvement. As one put it, "The whole cabinet decision-making system is very much a grass-roots dominated system ... genuine participation [by MLAs] is seen as the backbone of the system."

In addition, though, the impetus for such innovation and experimentation owes a good deal to Alberta's historical deviation from traditional Westminster patterns. The province's all-but-constant record of one-party dominance, which typically produces overwhelming government majorities in the legislature, combined with a strong populist streak in the political culture, has resulted in an openness to unconventional governance models, especially with respect to blurring the usually rigid demarcation between cabinet and government backbench (Englemann 1989). (The frequent recourse to formal votes in cabinet and standing policy committees – rare if not unknown in other cabinet processes – also illustrates the influence of Alberta's populist political culture.)

British Columbia's political culture also exhibits pronounced populist streaks, and although its party system was long competitive, the 2001 provincial election produced an Alberta-style landslide, with the Liberals capturing seventy-seven of seventy-nine seats. Among the innovations introduced by the victorious Liberals was a set of cabinet-caucus committees inspired by the Alberta model. As in Alberta, the five sectoral committees are chaired by private government members (with ministers as vice-chairs), and ministers are outnumbered by backbenchers.

The BC government caucus committees resemble their Alberta counterparts in size (twelve to sixteen members), the full access that all MLAs have to confidential cabinet documents in advance of meetings, and the practice of having committee chairs attend full cabinet meetings to present and explain committee reports on ministers' submissions (chairs participate in the discussion, remain for the decision, and then leave the cabinet meeting). Unlike in Alberta, votes are not taken; the committees operate by consensus, but backbench participation is said to be vigorous and genuine. The private members who chair committees have significant call upon central agency support; they are regularly briefed by Cabinet Office staff prior to meetings and have access to Treasury Board Secretariat fiscal analyses and staff if needed. In this they appear better served than their Alberta counterparts, who operate in an environment where central agencies figure much less prominently.

On the key question of what influence these government caucus committees afford BC backbenchers, we lack the detailed information required to attempt an answer. As in Alberta, however, private government members clearly do enjoy substantially greater access to critical documents and decision-making structures than in the more conventional governments elsewhere in Canada. By extension, they can hardly fail to have more policy clout.

It is not surprising that these notable departures from Westminster orthodoxy emerged in Alberta, where decades of single-party legislatures have powerfully shaped institutions and processes, and in British Columbia, long a breeding ground for eccentric politics. When tradition-bound, conventional Ontario follows suit, though, important psychological barriers to innovation have indeed been breached. On coming to power in late 2003, the McGuinty government established a series of Alberta-style cabinet committees, on which all Liberal private members serve. (This development is not shown in Table 4.4, which reports data collected prior to the Liberals' election.) Private members chair the six sectoral cabinet committees and lead cabinet discussions on proposals reviewed by the committees when they come before cabinet. On the critical Management Board and Priorities and Planning Board, private members are less in evidence: two "caucus advisors" sit on the former (membership on which is by statute limited to ministers), and the chair of the government caucus is a member of "P and P." "It's time to stop the practice of concentrating power in the hands of a few people in cabinet, or a few people in the Premier's Office," said McGuinty on unveiling the scheme. "When it comes to decision-making in our government, there will be no backbench" (Ontario Liberal Party 2003).

No definitive judgments can be offered on this brave assessment for some time. Early reaction, however, pointed up a potentially detrimental effect on democracy. One cynical opposition MPP claimed that the real intent of adding backbenchers to cabinet committees could be divined from the requirement that they take the cabinet oath of secrecy, which had the effect of "neutering and spaying all these new puppies here at Queen's Park in the hope that they won't get too frisky or chew at the furniture" (Peter Kormos quoted in Urquhart 2003a). It is indeed an open question whether (presumably) enhanced backbench participation in cabinet processes will come at the cost of emasculating legislative committees (hardly a concern in virtually oppositionless Alberta and British Columbia) and of inhibiting private members from criticizing their government in other public venues.

THE ROLE OF THE GOVERNMENT CAUCUS

Justifications of the strong party discipline that typically pervades Canadian legislatures routinely point to private members' influence in caucus as mitigating the apparent impotence of backbenchers vis-à-vis party leadership, especially on the government side of the House. Behind closed caucus doors, the argument runs, private members' views are expressed forthrightly and contribute meaningfully to policy decisions taken by the first minister and the cabinet. Few systematic evaluations of such claims have been attempted in Canada; the limited evidence available suggests that in isolated instances caucus can indeed be influential but overall lacks consistent clout. Paul Thomas, the leading Canadian analyst of party caucuses, has written of the federal caucus, "The primary role of the caucus in the governing party is to serve as a forum for communication and consultation ... [however,] in addition to helping shape the climate of opinion in which legislation is drafted, caucus discussions can lead to delay, modification, abandonment, and even rejection of bills presented by cabinet ministers" (Thomas 1996, 264-5). Both nationally and provincially the influence of caucus over government policy has increased perceptibly over the past few decades (Thomas 1998; Speaker 1998), but overall the government caucus remains a bit player on most issues most of the time.

The weakness of caucus reflects both raw power politics and institutional deficiencies. Those in the core executive with power are loath to share it. And typically the government caucus receives only limited information about proposed government initiatives (often late in the day) and moreover lacks a formal, routinized process for reviewing, let alone approving, cabinet proposals that would strengthen opportunities for involvement and influence.

The survey of Canadian practices reveals considerable variation in the mechanisms for (government) caucus review of cabinet initiatives and in the actual influence caucus can bring to bear. Table 4.5 presents the data in summary form. All government caucuses can expect cabinet to share with them some information about upcoming government policy before either legislation is introduced in the House or an initiative is announced publicly. Significant differences are evident, though, on several key questions. Do all substantive policies and legislative proposals come before caucus? Does caucus routinely have the opportunity to review proposals before or after cabinet has decided on them? Is caucus involvement largely limited to being informed of government plans by ministers, with few opportunities for questioning and criticism, or is formal caucus approval normally required before a draft bill or policy can go forward? (As discussed briefly below, caucus is quite a different institution and plays a fundamentally different role under consensus government in Nunavut and the Northwest Territories.)

In the largest legislatures – the House of Commons, the Quebec National Assembly, and the Ontario Legislature – caucus involvement tends to be weakest. Certainly some information, both pre- and post-cabinet decision, will be available to caucus, and some opportunities exist for closed-door discussions with ministers, especially on difficult or controversial issues. Nevertheless, although in these jurisdictions caucus objections have sometimes resulted in proposed government policy being extensively revised or even scuppered altogether, caucus normally lacks the capacity to pass judgment on policies going before cabinet. Exigencies of scale (and the associated press of business)

Table 4.5

Involvement of government caucus in cabinet decisions, 2002

Jurisdiction	
Newfoundland and Labrador	Some key policy issues are reviewed with caucus before cabinet takes decision.
Prince Edward Island	Premier consults government caucus on ad hoc basis when he wishes to obtain their views or inform them of rationale for cabinet decision.
Nova Scotia	Sensitive policy issues are typically vetted by government caucus before cabinet decision.
New Brunswick	All legislation must be approved by Caucus Committee on Legislation and reviewed by full caucus before introduction (occurs after cabinet consideration). Nonlegislative matters sometimes reviewed by caucus.
Quebec	Informal process, usually before cabinet decision.
Ontario	Government caucus committees advise ministers; ministers consult caucus on legislation before it goes to cabinet; other policies reviewed by caucus after cabinet decision.
Manitoba	Government caucus plays significant role in advance of legislation going to cabinet and also in priority setting. Some day-to-day cabinet decisions may be revisited by caucus if there is great concern over them.
Saskatchewan	Ministers review important decisions with government caucus, sometimes before, sometimes after they are considered by cabinet.
Alberta	All cabinet decisions are reported to government caucus. All proposed legislation is approved by caucus. Some nonlegislative policy referred by cabinet to caucus for approval. Review by caucus normally occurs after cabinet decision.
British Columbia	Government caucus reviews all legislation, except budget bills, before they are introduced in the House. Other matters may be referred by cabinet to caucus.
Yukon	Extensive caucus involvement in development of government legislation and policy.
Northwest Territories	Extensive role for "caucus" under consensus government.
Nunavut	Extensive role for "caucus" under consensus government.
Canada	Caucus plays variable role. No formal process for involvement in legislative or policy processes.

Source: Responses to author's questionnaire, 2002.

nationally and in the two largest provinces are evidently at play, but size is not determinative: the Ontario NDP government of the early 1990s developed a formal procedure by which the government caucus vetted draft legislation, with a clear understanding that proposed bills required caucus sanction (McDonald 1993; Christopherson 2003). Moreover, the legislature and the government caucus were larger than today's. Looking back some years later, a former NDP minister argued that strengthening the role of caucus in this way not only empowered backbenchers, but also improved legislation and tightened the bonds between cabinet and caucus (Christopherson 2003).

A comparison of practices in the Atlantic and Western provinces shows that political culture and a willingness to experiment with unconventional processes (which may of course be a function of political culture) are key to the role of the government caucus. In Atlantic Canada, the government caucus can undoubtedly become involved and influential on controversial issues, but this tends to occur on an ad hoc basis, often on the sufferance of the premier. Formal, regular mechanisms for caucus review of policy and legislation are absent. By contrast, in the West, especially in Manitoba and Alberta, formal caucus review of government legislation has been institutionalized and is seen as a normal part of the legislative process. No one harbours any illusions about cabinet's, and especially the premier's, ultimate authority to override caucus objections. A clear expectation has nonetheless been established of serious caucus review in the form of genuine opportunity to revise and on occasion reject draft legislation, not simply in being informed of important cabinet initiatives – though this is certainly important and not to be taken for granted.

The gist of this discussion has been that by virtue of institutional mechanisms and a more accommodating outlook, backbench involvement in policy making in the Western provinces is notably stronger than elsewhere in Canada. But unwarranted conclusions should not be drawn about how democratic and participatory cabinet processes are in these jurisdictions. First, the formal mechanisms for caucus review and approval apply only to legislation (and some jurisdictions exempt certain important legislation, such as budget bills). All sorts of far-reaching public policies can be realized without recourse to legislation, and on these, especially expenditure decisions, caucus involvement appears to be sporadic and ad hoc. In all jurisdictions, cabinet and the premier may refer nonlegislative policy issues for caucus consideration, but overall caucus influence is clearly significantly circumscribed. To an extent this is because the government caucus rarely has access to the information and bureaucratic expertise available to cabinet. As well, it reflects the primal fact that, for a variety of reasons, caucus cannot usually hope to do more than influence government policy by *reacting* to proposals emanating from cabinet; only in very general ways or unusual circumstances can caucus *initiate* policy or legislation. The net effect was well expressed by a government backbencher in Manitoba, who despite pronouncing himself generally pleased with caucus's capacity to amend or reject draft legislation, remarked, "We [government backbenchers] still feel like we're the B-team ... We're nobodies twenty feet from the caucus room."

In the consensus governments of the northern territories, caucus is a very different institution. In the absence of political parties, caucus consists of all MLAs, including ministers and the speaker, meeting regularly behind closed doors on substantial political issues. Cabinet unquestionably remains the centre of governmental power, but caucus is a crucial forum where private members and ministers can have frank discussions on difficult questions. Status distinctions between ministers and regular members are to be left at the door ("There are no ministers in Caucus" was how one MLA put it), and while it would be naïve to assume that anyone forgets who is and is not in cabinet, the ethos of equality among all MLAs is powerful. The significance of caucus waxes and wanes with any number of political factors. By times it is little more than a forum for the exchange of information and opinion, without the inhibiting transparency of the legislative chamber. On occasion, though, since private members outnumber ministers, caucus becomes a genuine decision-making body, with extensive private member participation and influence. Cabinet does not take orders from caucus and makes many decisions without consulting it, but most certainly takes caucus seriously, providing private members with significant, institutionalized involvement in cabinet decision making.

Just as the Nunavut/NWT model of consensus government is *sui generis*, so too the role of caucus in the North is unique. Its significance rests not only in its capacity to broaden democracy by giving elected MLAs access to cabinet but also in the way it demonstrates the range of possible mechanisms for legislative-executive interaction compatible with the Westminster model of responsible government.

Public Access to Cabinet Documents

If the public – or even its representatives – has very few opportunities to participate in the workings of cabinet, what of the transparency of the cabinet process? More specifically, does the public have access to cabinet documents that would shed light on how cabinet makes decisions and on the information and arguments it has before it when deciding an issue? A few decades ago cabinet secrecy was so pervasive this question would not have been worth asking. But in some recent instances, the veil of cabinet secrecy has been lifted before the documents in question have been rendered historical curiosities with no accountability value. Overall, though, has anything really changed? (While illicit cabinet leaks are always possible – indeed, photocopy machines and other modern technologies have greatly facilitated them – the focus here is on legal means of securing cabinet documents.) Let us examine the extent to which freedom of information processes, judicial decisions, and commissions of inquiry advance public access to cabinet documents.

Freedom of Information Legislation

The advent of freedom of information (FOI) legislation in the 1970s and 1980s marked a significant advance – symbolically and substantively – for democratic openness in Canadian government. The notion that citizens are legally entitled to great swaths of previously secret information held by government constitutes an important democratic reform. Attempts to chip away at FOI effectiveness through such ploys as charging prohibitively high fees and excluding privatized governmental functions or agencies from FOI provisions (Roberts 1999) are worrisome, but the essential value of FOI remains. In terms of access to cabinet documents, however, FOI makes only a limited contribution.

Though specific provisions vary, the fundamental elements of FOI regimes are similar across Canada, and a central premise of all Canadian legislation is that deliberations of cabinet are exempt from FOI processes. The language in the Alberta Freedom of Information and

Privacy Act is typical: "The head of a public body *must refuse* to disclose to an applicant information that would reveal the substance of deliberations of the Executive Council or any of its committees ... including any advice, recommendations, policy considerations or draft legislation or regulations submitted or prepared for submission" to cabinet or cabinet committees (s. 22[1], emphasis added). The Ontario act specifically exempts "an agenda, minute or other record of [cabinet or cabinet committee] deliberations" from FOI processes (s. 12[1][a]). Similar language is found in other jurisdictions.

While the prohibition against the release of documents that might reveal the "substance" of cabinet deliberations is severely limiting, it does not eliminate all possibilities. FOI commissioners, the independent officers of Parliament or the legislature who adjudicate appeals of government refusals to release information, have interpreted this provision as implying more than simply the subject of a cabinet discussion, setting a slightly lower standard for the release of documents. A 1995 court judgment upheld an Ontario Information and Privacy Commission ruling that the government provide solid evidence, as opposed to a mere assertion, that a document actually was the subject of consultation among ministers and would disclose the substance of cabinet deliberations (*Ontario* v. *Fineberg* 1995).

This decision demonstrates an important feature of FOI legislation. Wide exemptions provide grounds for governments to refuse to disclose cabinet documents. But FOI laws also require a government to justify to an independent commission its claim that this exemption applies to the document that has been requested. After reviewing the document and the government's argument, the commission renders a decision, which may be appealed to the courts. In other words, governments cannot simply claim an exemption; they must provide convincing evidence to a neutral adjudicative body. A major exception to this principle is the federal Access to Information Act, under which the clerk of the Privy Council (the cabinet secretary and highest-ranking public servant) can certify that a document qualifies as a cabinet record and is therefore exempt from release via FOI, effectively ending the process with no involvement of the federal commission.

FOI legislation usually allows for "severing" of documents, that is, release of portions of documents that are separated from nondisclosed documents (for example, a statistical appendix to a policy report). Even so, decisions by FOI commissioners have left little wiggle room for enterprising FOI users to finesse the cabinet document exemption by cleverly framing information requests to take advantage of the severability principle. Indeed, FOI commissioners have been very conservative in requiring release of documents severed from cabinet submissions or other materials. In one Ontario decision, for example, a request for a copy of a public opinion poll that formed the basis of a cabinet submission, but was not itself formally presented to cabinet, was denied on the grounds that it was used by ministers in their deliberations (Ontario Information and Privacy Commission 1993). The intriguing question of how releasing a factual report examining public opinion on an issue might betray what was said in cabinet is less important than the clear indication that FOI cannot be used to winkle cabinet documents out of government.

It is certainly possible, and indeed perhaps quite useful, for citizens to acquire information that cabinet had available to it in reaching a particular decision. Under the Alberta act, for example, "background facts" presented to cabinet may be released under FOI once the decision has been made public or implemented. But having the background facts — note "facts," not bureaucratic advice or political opinion — is hardly a major advance in knowing what went on in cabinet. And even here, an apparently technical change in the format of cabinet submissions in Ottawa sharply reduced the possibilities for making background material public by severing it from the documents containing advice and recommendations. In 1984, shortly after passage of the federal access law, the discussion papers prepared for cabinet (which are subject to FOI requests) were incorporated into the analysis section of the "memoranda to cabinet" in order to render them immune from FOI processes. A recent decision of the Federal Court of Canada rejected this ploy (*Minister of Environment* v. *Information Commission of Canada* [2003]). The government's appeal to the Federal Court of Appeal failed and, in the words of the federal information commissioner, the court "ordered the Clerk of the Privy Council to begin respecting the will of Parliament ... by disclosing the records or portions of records which contain the background, problem analysis and policy options presented to Cabinet for decision-making purposes" (Information Commissioner of Canada 2003, 11).

Not all FOI processes are so hamstrung by legal restrictions. The Nova Scotia act, though hardly declaring open season on cabinet documents, is in certain respects notably more accommodating than other Canadian FOI regimes. In the important *O'Connor* decision – on an FOI request brought by staff of opposition MLAs – the Nova Scotia Court of Appeal affirmed that the unique provisions of the province's Freedom of Information and Protection of Privacy Act limit the grounds for denying the release of cabinet documents when an FOI request is made. While clearly maintaining cabinet confidentiality as an important principle restricting the availability of cabinet documents, the court adopted a relatively narrow approach to determining which documents should not be released. The decision endorsed the view of the lower court judge who had ruled at an earlier stage of the case that "cabinet may base its deliberations on a variety of data, some of which deserve no protection [from FOI requests] at all" (*O'Connor* v. *Nova Scotia* 2001). The Supreme Court of Canada denied the province's request to appeal the decision.

Paradoxically, this important decision affirming Nova Scotians' unusually broad legal rights to certain cabinet documents confirms restrictions on the ability of other Canadians to gain access to cabinet documents through FOI processes. The court of appeal made it clear that its ruling rested on provisions of the Nova Scotia act that have no equivalent elsewhere in Canada (*O'Connor* v. *Nova Scotia* 2001, par. 54-6). The act's purposes are set out in the following unequivocal way: "to ensure that public bodies are *fully accountable* to the public" and "to provide for the disclosure of *all government information*" subject only to exemptions that are "necessary ... limited and specific" (s. 2, emphasis added). These provisions are designed to facilitate a number of good-governance objectives including "informed public participation in policy formulation ... fairness in government decision-making

... [and] the airing and reconciliation of divergent views" (s. 2). No other Canadian FOI regime has similar language.

While the *O'Connor* decision has perceptibly enhanced the Nova Scotia government's propensity to release parts of cabinet documents that it would have previously declared entirely exempt under FOI, cabinet confidentiality remains the norm, and a very strong norm at that. Even the remarkably direct and forceful language of the Nova Scotia FOI act has not fundamentally altered the reach of cabinet secrecy. By extension, were other Canadian jurisdictions to adopt the standards of the Nova Scotia act, the results might be noteworthy but would hardly constitute a serious threat to the maintenance of cabinet confidentiality.

The *O'Connor* decision illustrates that the courts can be valuable allies in the quest for access to cabinet documents. Do they indeed represent a way to breach the ramparts of cabinet secrecy?

JUDICIAL DECISIONS

Not all judicial decisions on disclosure of cabinet documents have been generated by disputes over FOI requests. A number of important cases have arisen from legal actions taken by citizens or organizations against governments, which have entailed requests for access to cabinet documents or for ministers to testify in public settings.

Without becoming entangled in detailed analysis of judicial decisions turning on arcane and complex legal arguments, some overall conclusions can be offered. First, the courts have come to recognize that cabinet secrecy, though a central and appropriate feature of Canadian government, is not absolute. In the 1986 *Carey* decision, the Supreme Court of Canada noted that cabinet confidentiality can collide with the justice system's need for full information and observed that "the general balance between these two competing interests has shifted markedly over the years," adding that "the need for secrecy in government operations may vary with the particular public interest sought to be protected" (*Carey* v. *Ontario* 1986, par. 22-3). In this noteworthy case, the Court flatly rejected the submission of the Ontario cabinet secretary that cabinet documents should be covered by an unquestioned blanket nondisclosure principle simply by virtue of being cabinet documents. In the Court's view, the passage of time was a key, though not definitive, consideration in determining whether cabinet documents could be made public (the case, which went to trial in 1982, involved a request for cabinet documents from 1973 and 1974). Subsequent Supreme Court decisions have confirmed the principles enunciated in *Carey*.

The crucial question of whether ministers can be compelled to testify about cabinet decisions was determined by the Supreme Court in the case of *Smallwood* v. *Sparling*. Former Newfoundland premier Joey Smallwood had been called to testify in a Restrictive Trade Practices Commission inquiry into a company that had had extensive dealings with his government. Smallwood's stance that the doctrine of cabinet secrecy overrode any public interest argument and afforded him a blanket immunity against testifying about cabinet business was decisively rejected. The Court did not specify what limits might apply to his testimony – and certainly did not support the position that all ministers could be forced to testify in all circumstances – but it did cite approvingly the principle set out in a leading British case that "the court should intervene [to uphold claims for cabinet secrecy] only in the clearest of cases where the continuing confidentiality of the material can be demonstrated" (*Attorney-General* v. *Jonathan Cape Ltd.* [1975] quoted in *Smallwood* v. *Sparling* 1982, 707).

If this discussion suggests that favourable court rulings are unlocking the secrets of cabinet, a second look strongly tempers any such interpretation. Although the courts have shown themselves willing to consider, and under certain circumstances authorize, the public release of cabinet documents, this has almost always been in the interests of legal rather than political pursuits. In other words, litigants (primarily those in legal battles with government) who claim that secret cabinet documents contain evidence essential for a just resolution of their cases may find the courts prepared to support them. Those seeking cabinet documents for political reasons, however ("political" being broadly defined to encompass a number of public policy objectives), cannot expect such favourable treatment from the courts.

A more general conclusion follows. While primacy of the rule of law – a central precept of any democratic system – may on occasion require the disclosure in open court of cabinet documents to ensure justice in legal proceedings, the prospects for advancing democracy by broadening public access to cabinet documents through the courts are slight.

Public Inquiries

In a few recent high-profile cases cabinet documents – sometimes very current ones – have been requested, received, and made public by royal commissions or public inquiries. Nova Scotia's royal commission into the wrongful conviction of Donald Marshall in the 1980s and the public inquiries into the tainted water catastrophes in Walkerton, Ontario, and North Battleford, Saskatchewan, in 2000-2 are perhaps the best-known illustrations.

The Walkerton inquiry developed an elaborate protocol by which its staff reviewed, circulated to lawyers for involved parties, and entered into evidence all manner of confidential material including cabinet documents and the personal files of the premier's political staff. Commission staff reviewed hundreds of thousands of government documents and eventually scanned about 200,000 into an electronic database, which was provided to parties to the inquiry. Officials of the parties signed confidentiality agreements. A great many documents unearthed by the commission were never made public, not because the government claimed cabinet privilege applied to them (which it did for a small number of documents), but because they were deemed not relevant to the inquiry (for details see O'Connor 2002, ch. 14). Substantial numbers of cabinet documents were entered into evidence and thus made public. As well, ministers were questioned extensively about discussions in cabinet and about conversations between ministers and between ministers and staff. These documents and this testimony presented a singular portrait of the Harris cabinet and its decision-making processes and priorities – a portrait that not surprisingly generated tremendous media attention.

Remarkable as it was for the public to hear about the inner workings of cabinet on an issue of utmost public concern, public inquiries are not models for more wide-ranging release of cabinet documents. Not only are such occurrences rare and limited in their scope to specific episodes or policies, but they come into existence (and enjoy broad terms of reference authorizing review and release of cabinet documents) only with the agreement of the government.

Public inquiries can and do bring into the public domain sensitive and important cabinet documents. Moreover, the precedents set by the Marshall, Walkerton, and other inquiries – that in instances of grievous government errors or horrendous tragedies, normal restrictions on cabinet documents must give way – add in important ways to cabinet accountability. Overall, however, such inquiries are far removed from the routine matters on which citizens, organizations, or politicians would want access to cabinet documents.

THE CASE FOR SECRECY

Cabinet documents are not forever veiled in secrecy, at least not in all Canadian jurisdictions. In Ottawa and most provinces and territories, even the most sensitive cabinet documents are eventually sent to the archives and made available to the public. Every January, Library and Archives Canada releases minutes of cabinet meetings under the thirty-year rule. While the record of cabinet deliberations can be illuminating – it was nothing short of fascinating to read in 2001 who said what in cabinet during the October Crisis of 1970 – access to historical cabinet records does nothing to further democratic accountability or participation. Availability also varies a good deal: in Nova Scotia, archived cabinet documents are generally available after ten years; in Nunavut and Yukon, the threshold is fifteen years; Ontario has a twenty-year rule; other jurisdictions follow Ottawa's thirty-year embargo; and Alberta and the Northwest Territories lack formal procedures for archiving cabinet documents.

Cabinet can of course choose to release documents of its own accord. Indeed, FOI legislation typically makes provision for this possibility when requests are made for cabinet documents that would otherwise be exempt from FOI processes, but in practice this has proven unworkable. In British Columbia, documents associated with open cabinet meetings – agendas, submissions, transcripts, and the like – are posted on the Internet. Though some of this information is doubtless of value to interested citizens and organizations, just as the open cabinet meetings are not genuine exercises in decision making, these documents seem unlikely to contain the confidential material on which cabinet bases its debates and decisions.

Overall, while notable exceptions may be cited, it is clear that whether the vehicle is the FOI regime, judicial decisions, or commissions of inquiry, the road to public disclosure of cabinet documents comes to a dead end. Aside from the ubiquitous but unsystematic leaks that characterize any cabinet, precious few opportunities exist for the citizenry to gain access to cabinet documents before they become historical artifacts with zero value in terms of political accountability or transparency. Does this constitute a significant restriction for the prospects of attaining genuine democracy in Canadian governance?

Not at all. To be sure, the Nova Scotia experience demonstrates that room exists to enhance public access to background information on which cabinet decisions are made, for example through more muscular FOI regimes. Yet good governance would not be served by wholesale publication of cabinet submissions and minutes. Transparency and ready access to information are critical elements of good democratic governance, but not the only ones. Cabinet could simply not operate effectively if its deliberations, the advice it receives, and the decisions it makes were subject to being made public while the matters in question were still in the public eye. The Ontario FOI act contains a "public interest override," replicated in other FOI regimes, whereby a compelling public interest trumps certain exemptions on release of information; significantly, however, it does not apply to cabinet documents. Clearly, the FOI-exempt status of cabinet documents allows ministers to hide all manner of unpalatable and embarrassing positions and ideas. Yet requiring disclosure of cabinet records would compromise cabinet secrecy and undermine the ability of ministers to speak freely in cabinet and of officials to advise ministers frankly. Cabinet secrecy is not just a convenient political dodge; it is essential to effective government, not least in serving as a necessary precondition for the central constitutional principle of cabinet solidarity.

The courts – admittedly conservative institutions, but institutions nonetheless adept at rendering balanced judgments on difficult issues – have spoken eloquently on the need for cabinet confidentiality, and not just in ethereal constitutional terms but as a practical necessity. In the *Babcock* decision the Supreme Court observed, "Cabinet confidentiality is essential to good government ... those charged with the heavy responsibility of making government decisions must be free to discuss all aspects of the problem that come before them and to express all manner of views, without fear that what they read, say or act on will later be subject to public scrutiny" (*Babcock* v. *Canada [A.G.]*, [2002], par. 15, 18).

Some years earlier the Court quoted with approval a leading British case on the need for cabinet confidentiality and thus the inadvisability of public release of cabinet documents: "Such disclosure would create or fan ill-informed or captious public or political criticism. The business of government is difficult enough as it is, and no government could contemplate with equanimity the inner workings of the government machine being exposed to the gaze of those ready to criticise without adequate knowledge of the background and perhaps with some axe to grind" (*Conway* v. *Rimmer* quoted in *Carey* v. *Ontario* 1986, par. 49).

Cabinet As Appeal Body

From time to time, Canadian cabinets perform the role of appeal bodies, hearing and deciding on formal petitions to overturn or amend decisions of semi-independent government agencies such as the Canadian Radio-television and Telecommunications Commission (CRTC) in Ottawa and the Environmental Appeal Board in British Columbia.

Might this practice offer an avenue for public access to cabinet and participation in its processes? In words of one syllable, no.

Most Canadian jurisdictions do not permit appeals to cabinet from decisions of quasi-judicial bodies. (As a leading administrative law text points out, technically these requests for cabinet to overturn or vary tribunal decisions are petitions rather than appeals, because the latter term implies a legal avenue with clearly set out procedures and requirements of natural justice, public records, and so forth, which are entirely absent [Macaulay 2003, 28-2-3].) And where appeals are possible, they are infrequent or unknown. In five provinces and two territories, cabinet secretaries indicated that neither cabinet nor cabinet committees receive appeals; in another province and another territory, officials were reluctant to say definitively that no appeals were possible but believed this to be the case and were unable to recollect any specific instances of appeals. In the provinces that do permit appeals to cabinet (in Ontario, cabinet committee), only a very small number of the myriad semi-independent agencies are subject to having their decisions formally appealed to cabinet, and at that on fairly restricted grounds. Such appeals are uncommon: in British Columbia, three or four years may elapse between them; in Quebec only a very few occurred in the previous decade. The Ontario cabinet received about forty petitions a year in the early 1980s (Ontario Management Board of Cabinet 1989, 9-67), but that number has declined significantly, especially since appeals to cabinet of the often controversial decisions of the Ontario Municipal Board were abolished. Finally, when cabinets do receive and adjudicate formal appeal petitions, they uniformly do so on the basis of written submissions; neither the petitioners nor their legal representatives are permitted to appear in person before cabinet.

The glimmer of democracy by way of appeals against decisions of semi-independent agencies turns out to be a will-o'-the-wisp. Does this represent a loss of a potentially valuable use of cabinet to enhance democracy? Perhaps, but some would argue that permitting cabinet to overturn decisions of independent semi-judicial agencies constitutes not an advance but a perversion of democracy. Political interference with processes of natural justice, through cabinet fiat, would not be tolerated in the judicial system, so why should independent, quasi-judicial bodies be subject to such intrusions?

Public Participation through Public Representatives

Save in the most limited ways, the Canadian public does not participate in cabinet processes. Nor can it observe what goes on in cabinet and cabinet committees, or obtain much in the way of formal documentation about cabinet deliberations. A few minor advances have occurred in recent years, such as occasional access to cabinet documents through FOI processes and public inquiries, and interest group delegations to cabinet, but overall, Canadian cabinets are exclusionary in the extreme and operate behind an almost totally opaque veil of secrecy.

More open and transparent cabinets might well be more democratic in a mechanistic way, but genuine decision making at the apex of government cannot be expected to take place before the public's gaze, with full recording of the real substance of discussions leading to the decisions. Cabinet secrecy can be seen as a necessary evil in the pursuit of good decision making and good governance.

Does this chapter thus end with the elitist and fatalistic message that cabinet must necessarily remain highly undemocratic in its isolation from both public involvement and public scrutiny? Is our conclusion that public access is neither possible nor desirable? Not necessarily. The key lies in the recognition that cabinet is not an institution of populist or direct democracy but of representative democracy. If the question is reframed from "Can the public participate?" to "Can the public's representatives participate?" the chapter suggests that positive, democratic – though less than tectonic – change is possible.

In several jurisdictions backbench government members participate far more actively in cabinet processes than has traditionally been supposed. We need not buy into the rhetoric of sweeping backbench influence to conclude that meaningful involvement of private (government) members can occur through formal mechanisms for caucus review of proposed policy and legislation or through active member-ship on cabinet committees. The lack of definitive data on how these processes work in the provinces where they are in place should make us cautious in accepting their democratic potential, but not dismis-sive. Nor should we be alarmed that the sacred canons of responsible Westminster government have been somehow compromised by such developments. As has been repeatedly stressed in this book, the West-minster system is wonderfully flexible, admitting of many substantial variations. The innovations reviewed in this chapter pale in their apparent lack of orthodoxy by comparison with the hybrid National Assembly for Wales, where legislative and executive structures and functions are uniquely intermingled (Laffin and Thomas 2000; 2001).

Chapter 4

Strengths

- Cabinets, mainly at the provincial-territorial level, travel outside the capital to meet with citizens and interest groups. Even though such travel is largely intended to promote the government's political agenda, it can have positive benefits in linking the citizenry to the top decision makers.

- In some jurisdictions, government backbenchers participate meaningfully in cabinet processes, especially in cabinet committees.

- In some jurisdictions, the government caucus is meaningfully involved in cabinet decision-making processes, especially with regard to proposed legislation.

- The advent of freedom of information laws and the occasional judicial inquiry or court decision have permitted some limited public access to cabinet documents.

- Cabinet secrecy, and the resultant limitations on public access to cabinet documents, is not inherently evil or dangerous. Lack of confidentiality could seriously impede decision making, which often requires tough and frank debate among ministers and their advisors.

Weaknesses

- The possibilities of well-organized interest groups, let alone individual citizens, appearing before cabinet or cabinet committees are, at best, remote.

- In general, government backbenchers, both as individual members and collectively as caucus, have little influence on cabinet decisions and minimal involvement in formal cabinet processes.

- Public access to cabinet documents is more limited than it needs to be to preserve the principle of cabinet secrecy.

5

DEMOCRACY THROUGH CABINET STRUCTURE AND PROCESS?

Chapter 4 looked at participation in formal cabinet discussions and at the possibilities for public access to cabinet and its documents. This chapter broadens the inquiry by looking at core executive structure and process, including internal cabinet operations. Whereas the previous chapter was largely restricted to discussion of the cabinet proper, this chapter examines how other components of the core executive contribute to Canadian democracy or detract from it. Central topics are the size and formal structure of cabinet, the nature and role of central agency officials and partisan staff, the representational imperative, and executive federalism.

Virtually every aspect of core executive structure and process appears to have both positive and negative influences on democracy. The judgments offered in this chapter about net enhancements or reductions of democracy are necessarily speculative; far more extensive study than is attempted here would be required to reach definitive answers.

Cabinet Structure

For our purposes, the principal issues of cabinet structure relate to size, internal structure (most notably the question of formal cabinet tiers), cabinet committees, and the extent of cabinet bureaucratization.

SIZE

As noted in Chapter 2, Canadian cabinets are unusually large. As with other aspects of cabinet structure and process, while the implications for democracy of a cabinet's size may not be immediately apparent, they may be teased out. On balance, larger cabinets are conducive to enhanced democracy, though the effects are probably limited.

In terms of the key criterion of participation, large cabinets clearly involve more people directly in government decision making. In turn this can only widen the range of interests and perspectives brought to bear. Given that our system is one of representative democracy, the larger the number of elected representatives with a meaningful say in decisions the better. This is not to imply that all ministers in a large cabinet have substantial clout. Indeed, junior or newly appointed ministers can find themselves at some distance from real power literally and figuratively. (New ministers are typically assigned seats at the end of the cabinet table, so distant from the first minister that some complain, to researchers at least, that they can barely hear the discussion.) Nonetheless, ministers are undeniably more powerful than private members; they are more involved in decisions, with better access to information and resources.

In *Legislatures,* his volume for the Democratic Audit, David Docherty (2004) demonstrates that increasing the size of Canadian legislatures would contribute to democratizing them. One of his central arguments is that robust legislative committee systems – important for maximizing legislatures' democratic potential – require sufficient numbers of MPs or MLAs. A similar logic applies to cabinets.

Although an effective cabinet committee system does not require a large number of ministers, larger cabinets become so unwieldy and inefficient as decision-making bodies that they necessarily delegate substantial authority to committees. This is potentially significant for democracy since, as discussed below, recourse to cabinet committees produces more collegial decisions in which greater numbers of ministers have a genuine say.

Not all consequences of increased cabinet size constitute enhancements to democracy. The literature on small groups suggests that "as the group becomes larger, the demands on the leader's role become greater and more numerous, and tolerance for leader-centred direction of group activities becomes greater" (Shaw 1981, 170-1). Thus while a large cabinet may well require strong political management skills on the first minister's part, it also strengthens his or her position by palpably diminishing the prospects that a small group of powerful ministers can carry the day in cabinet over the first minister's wishes. For first ministers inclined to use them, opportunities for divide and conquer tactics are also greater. Moreover, other things being equal, any given single minister has less influence vis-à-vis the first minister in a larger cabinet. In short, to the extent that reducing the constraints on the first minister's power is undemocratic, larger cabinets can represent a diminution of democracy. Overall, however, larger cabinets hold greater democratic potential than small ones, though the differences seem modest.

SINGLE-TIER CABINETS

Save a few recent examples, Canadian cabinets are not formally tiered, with layers of cabinet and noncabinet ministers, as is the norm in Australia and Britain. The implications for democracy of tiered cabinet structures are straightforward and potentially substantial. Restricting access to critical cabinet processes, most notably but not exclusively cabinet meetings themselves, to an elite inner cabinet is hardly democratic. The exclusion of noncabinet ministers can encompass not only formal access to meetings and information but also informal norms limiting their participation. The Australian experience, for example, demonstrates that even when noncabinet ministers attend cabinet during consideration of items within their purview, "they do feel inhibited about entering discussion too fully" (Weller 1980, 607).

Of course, all but the smallest cabinets exhibit clear (if fluid) pecking orders of ministers. Even in the absence of a formally constituted inner cabinet (often in the form of a priorities and planning committee), virtually every first minister depends heavily on an informal inner cabinet of especially strong and able colleagues, who wield extensive power. Still, institutionalizing the divide between cabinet ministers and lesser, noncabinet ministers, especially when junior ministers report to senior ministers, is not a particularly democratic way of organizing the core executive.

To some extent, judgments as to the democratic implications of tiered core executives depend on the trade-offs between proximity to real decision-making power and number of ministers. Since we are concerned about inclusiveness and participation, an untiered cabinet of thirty-five, beyond which few government members experience much genuine involvement in cabinet processes, is less democratic than a tiered ministry, in which the cabinet numbers just twenty but another thirty or forty junior ministers exercise substantial influence, even without the status of full cabinet membership.

If the restrictions imposed by tiered cabinets on ministerial participation in cabinet processes constitute a debit in the democratic ledger, there is an entry on the credit side, albeit not perhaps of the same magnitude. Establishing an inner tier of senior ministers, under whom junior ministers serve, makes for enhanced accountability. Simply put, a clear hierarchy of senior and junior ministers makes it easier to determine who is in charge and who should be held to account for government errors and omissions.

On balance, formally tiered ministries may be rational and efficient, but they are less inclusive and permit less participation and are therefore less democratic than untiered cabinets.

CABINET COMMITTEES

Our premise here is that cabinet committees are active and effective; cabinet committees that exist largely on paper are of no interest in this discussion. On balance, vigorous cabinet committee systems can contribute significantly to democratizing cabinet decision making. The essential calculus is that recourse to committees substantially widens the number of ministers with meaningful involvement in important decisions. Initially this seems counterintuitive: shouldn't full cabinet, where all ministers can take part in debate, provide a better venue for ministerial participation than a committee, where only a few ministers are involved in decision making? Indeed so for any single decision. When all ministers take part in deliberations, however, the more inclusive participation in individual decisions comes at the cost of limited or no participation in other decisions for which full cabinet has no time. In other words, more ministers can participate extensively in more decisions – and not simply leave them to the responsible departmental minister or the first minister – through a muscular committee system. (As discussed in Chapter 4, the combined cabinet-caucus committees in Alberta, British Columbia, and Ontario permit significant backbench participation in decision making.)

Much depends on the rules – formal and informal – by which cabinet committees operate. Exceptions occur, but the trend across Canada and in other Anglo-Celtic Westminster systems has increasingly been for full cabinet to accept, with little or no debate, the decisions or recommendations of cabinet committees. Typically a minister objecting to a committee decision can ask to have it reviewed by full cabinet, but this is not a common occurrence. Acceptance is certainly expedient – much of the rationale for committees is lost when their discussions are rehashed at full cabinet – but it can be undemocratic in that ministers who are not members of committees are effectively excluded from important decisions. In turn ministers' commitment to the crucial principle of cabinet solidarity could decline if they are consistently asked to take responsibility for decisions in which they had little or no say. These objections, however, are less problematic than the alternative to widespread cabinet committee activity: a far higher proportion of decisions effectively being made by individual ministers for want of time in full cabinet. (Similar logic suggests that, by virtue of the wide range of experience and insight that committees of ministers can bring to bear, decisions made by cabinet committees are likely to be better decisions than those taken by a single minister, but that is not our concern here.)

In terms of opening up cabinet processes to public participation, committees offer greater potential than full cabinet for travel and direct interaction with groups and individuals. The evidence of Chapter 4, however, is that the opportunities for cabinet committee interaction with the public or with organized interests are largely unrealized in Canada.

What of the first minister's power in a strong cabinet committee system? It is well to recall that the first minister controls the membership, leadership, mandate, and in fact the very existence of cabinet committees. The first minister may choose, as Prime Minister Martin did at the outset of his term, to chair key cabinet committees himself. Cabinet committee membership and the flow of committee business can be manipulated by determined first ministers so as to increase their influence. Margaret Thatcher was infamous for stacking committees with supportive ministers and steering problematic decisions their way. Similarly, some seasoned observers of the Ottawa scene contend that Prime Minister Trudeau's creation of an active, extensive cabinet committee system substantially enhanced his power, since the effective decision-making site for many important issues shifted from individual ministers' offices, which had largely operated beyond the prime ministers' gaze, to a committee system firmly controlled by the prime minister and his staff. Patrick Weller maintains that, as a general proposition, expansion of cabinet committee systems and the accompanying formalization of cabinet processes increase the first minister's power (Weller 1992b, 22).

In other important ways, though, a vigorous system of cabinet committees undercuts the first minister's power by reducing his or her capacity to impose decisions. Instead of simply directing an isolated,

individual minister, the first minister has to take on a group of ministers who are knowledgeable and committed and collectively carry more
political clout. Of course, as noted in Chapter 3, on any given issue the
first minister can best any group of ministers, but the political costs of
overruling or pre-empting a group of ministers may be considerable.
Moreover, for many of the specific issues coming before cabinet committees, the first minister lacks the time or inclination to become
involved.

These questions about whether extensive recourse to cabinet committees enhances or constrains the first minister's power vis-à-vis
individual ministers or groups of ministers cannot be answered in the
abstract. In present-day Canada, when the press of public business and
the complexity of the decisions at issue are so great, much depends on
the information and oversight resources available to cabinet and to the
first minister. Otherwise put, the scope and capacity of central agencies (discussed below) have a powerful bearing on the power relations
between the first minister and his or her cabinet colleagues, strong
committee system or no.

BUREAUCRATIZATION

The hallmark of the modern Canadian cabinet is a complex, highly routinized set of formal procedures for decision making. Even the smallest provinces and territories produce detailed manuals setting out at
length the processes to be followed in submitting a matter to cabinet
or cabinet committee, the deadlines to be met, and the forms to be completed with detailed information on costs, political and administrative
implications, communications plans, records of consultations with
stakeholders and other government departments, and so on. To be
sure, the formalities are sometimes ignored, though as a rule only with
the first minister's approval (indeed, the first minister is often the
worst offender). Clearly, however, the norm is one of comprehensive,
formal bureaucratic processes, supervised and enforced by powerful
central agencies.

As noted in Chapter 2, this is a relatively recent development. As late as the 1970s some provinces lacked formal cabinet agendas or official minutes recording cabinet decisions; processes for bringing matters to cabinet attention were often haphazard and failed to give ministers the information they needed or enough time to consider it. Moreover, in jurisdictions that have had established routines for cabinet decision making for some time, the clear trend is toward increased formality and bureaucratization. By way of illustration, cabinet submission guidelines not only specify what information is required, they prescribe the font and type size in which it is to be presented.

Is all this of interest to anyone not obsessed with the minutiae of government operations? Has it any bearing on questions of cabinet democracy? Indeed it does. Routinized formal processes are essential to the efficiency of cabinet and, by extension, government – massive, multibillion-dollar organizations require nothing less. Efficiency and democracy are sometimes antithetical goals, but in this instance they coincide, because order fosters democracy. The essential purpose of the formalization of cabinet processes is to ensure that ministers are in a position to participate effectively in cabinet decision making. This requires that they have sufficient information on the issues at hand, that they have time to review the information, reflect on it, and seek advice if necessary, and that they have the opportunity to contribute to important decisions for which they will be held responsible. When these conditions are met, more ministers are able to participate meaningfully. This makes for greater inclusion and a wider representation of interests and viewpoints in decision making as well as better-informed deliberation.

Additionally, to the extent that ministers' capacity to make informed decisions is improved, the discretion left to bureaucrats is lessened. In other words, effective decision-making power shifts from the unelected to the elected officials – a clear gain for democracy. Bringing about just such a reform was a major motivation behind Trudeau's reorganization of cabinet processes in Ottawa.

Finally, more formal bureaucratic cabinet processes generate a great deal of paper. Chapter 4 demonstrated how limited is the public's ability to gain access to cabinet documents, but in some circumstances some cabinet documents can be made public. The net gain for transparency and accountability may thus be marginal, but a gain it is.

It needs to be said by way of reality check that the *possibilities* set out above for enhancing democracy through cabinet bureaucratization are not always realized. Ministers are extraordinarily busy with staggering amounts of paper crossing their desks and often lack the time, inclination, or ability to digest and use the material made available to them.

On the other side of the ledger are the downsides for democracy resulting from cabinet bureaucratization. The possibility that more formal processes will increase the first minister's power has already been mentioned. More significant perhaps, though the goal may be ensuring that key decisions are in the hands of elected ministers rather than unelected bureaucrats, the politicians may well lose power to the bureaucrats, especially those in the central agencies. Bureaucrats generally have the advantage over ministers in manoeuvring through complex administrative processes. Moreover, bureaucrats who perform the crucial gatekeeping function, such as deciding when submissions from ministers and departments meet the criteria for cabinet consideration, can wield enormous power. The line between bureaucratic advice in support of ministers and bureaucratic subversion of ministerial priorities through control of the process may be thin indeed. The more complex the processes, the greater the potential for power to flow from the elected politicians to the unelected bureaucrats, thereby undermining democracy. And in departmentalized cabinets, in which ministers individually rather than cabinet collectively make decisions, the danger exists of unelected officials capturing individual ministers, usurping their power.

In sum, formalization of cabinet processes produces both pluses and minuses in the democratization column, but the bottom line is a positive number: democracy is better served when rigorous bureaucratic routines are in place and enforced.

Central Agencies

The effect of central agencies on the health of Canadian democracy is an important but complex question. At first blush, it might seem obvious that the remarkable growth in the scope and influence of central agencies in recent decades represents a baneful development for Canadian democracy. After all, Donald Savoie's important book, *Governing from the centre* (1999), which puts the case forcefully about what its subtitle calls "the concentration of power in Canadian politics," devotes extensive attention to the growing clout of Ottawa's central agencies. Long-time observers of the Ottawa scene argue that the prime minister is not notably more powerful today than his predecessors of four and five decades past, but that the accretion of bureaucratic power within the central agencies over the same time span is nothing short of remarkable. Massive centralization of power, they suggest, has indeed taken place within the federal government but at the bureaucratic rather than the political level.

With the evidence so clear, how can any verdict save "undemocratic" be rendered? Other things being equal, concentrated power diminishes democracy. Of the key democratic values highlighted in the Democratic Audit, participation and inclusiveness are ill served by concentrated power, while responsiveness and transparency are unlikely to be advanced, though accountability may be enhanced. But are other things really equal? Much depends on how the power shift entailed in the rise of central agencies is interpreted, especially as regards the influence of bureaucrats on politicians.

Before examining this question, let us briefly reprise the discussion in Chapter 2 as to what central agencies are and what they do. Central agencies are small but powerful government departments that concentrate almost exclusively on internal government operations, as opposed to delivering services and programs to the public. They are well placed strategically by virtue of their close and constant interaction with cabinet and its committees – senior central agency staff are the only non-ministers regularly present at cabinet and cabinet committee meetings – and with especially powerful politicians, such as the first minister and the finance minister. Central agencies serve as gate-keepers to cabinet, guardians of cabinet decision-making processes, and valued advisors on matters of policy and politics. Large, powerful central agencies may be found in cabinet systems both simple and complex, but typically – some would say necessarily – the creation of an active, extensive cabinet committee system fosters substantial expansion in the size and capacity of central agencies.

The question of how growing central agency influence affects democracy largely turns on whether the prime beneficiaries of this transformation are the elected politicians or the appointed bureau-crats. Accordingly, we should recall a key distinction. Normally all but one of the central agencies are staffed by permanent officials and are bureaucratic in nature and outlook; these include the Privy Council/Cabinet/Executive Council Office, the Department of Finance, the Treasury/Management Board Secretariat, and the Department of Justice/Attorney General's Department. The exception is the formid-able Prime Minister's/Premier's Office, whose unabashedly political operatives provide explicitly partisan political advice and support to the first minister.

Clearly the advance of central agencies has come at the expense of line departments, whose capacity for independent action has been diminished. But who in those line departments has had their influence undermined by intrusive central agencies: the ministers or the bureau-crats? And who has seen their power enhanced: ministers collectively, the prime minister, or the central agency officials? If the elected politi-cians are more firmly in control – as a collective, rather than as indi-viduals – and the power of the appointed bureaucrats has been curtailed, this is a net gain for democracy. Even if the ministers rather than the bureaucrats had been the real decision makers at the line departments, to the extent that more muscular central agencies facili-tate more genuinely collective cabinet decision making, then partici-pation and inclusiveness have strengthened and with them democracy.

Savoie argues persuasively, though, that cabinet has lost power to central agencies and that any notion of cabinet becoming a more effective and collective decision-making body through central agency support misconstrues the key dynamic of central agency influence. "Substantive debate on a Cabinet proposal," he writes, "increasingly takes place between the sponsoring minister and his department and the central agency officials, who are often the only ones sufficiently well plugged in to a proposal to see it take shape, and who have the time and resources to focus both on the deck [Powerpoint-style summaries] and the memorandum [the detailed cabinet submission]" (Savoie 1999, 134).

By anyone's account, the power of one elected politician has been enhanced through the bulking up of central agencies: the prime minister. Disagreement exists on the question of how substantially the prime minister's position has been strengthened; Savoie contends that the accretion of power has been extensive, while others see a less dramatic shift. Still, adding yet more power to an already enormously powerful individual clearly diminishes democracy.

The central agencies have clearly contributed to the concentration of power at the centre, but is the centre a solid monolith or is it a shifting constellation of organizations and interests often at odds with one another? Conflict and competition among central agencies would make for less comprehensive, and thus less worrisome, concentration of power. Certainly key central agencies – PCO, PMO, and Finance in Ottawa – do indeed have different perspectives and interests, and their relationships can be marked by rivalry and tension that sometimes descend into serious confrontation and strife. At the same time, though, the principal figures in central agencies cooperate effectively, respect one another's sphere's of influence, and present a generally unified stance to those outside the centre (Savoie 1999, ch. 6). Where we might expect to find the greatest friction, in the linkage between the politicos in the PMO/Premier's Office and the bureaucrats in the PCO/Cabinet Office, the working relationship is often close and professional. The centre may not be monolithic, but the extent to which inter-agency dissension mitigates the concentration of power at the centre varies a good deal; the specific dynamics of central agency interaction for any given government is an empirical question, depending on a host of factors.

All told, then, Savoie's thesis about the growing concentration of power at the centre of government in Canada is difficult to dispute, though considerable room for disagreement exists as to how serious the problem is and the threat it poses to Canadian democracy. But Savoie writes only of Ottawa. How valid is his analysis at the provincial and territorial level?

Although no detailed, systematic comparative studies exist of the nature and influence of central agencies in the territories and provinces, two conclusions can be ventured. First, in some jurisdictions, powerful central agencies certainly do contribute substantially to the concentration of power around the premier and his or her top advisors. During the Clark regime in British Columbia, for example, a strongly politicized central agency, the Cabinet Policy and Communications Secretariat (CPCS, widely known as "cupcakes"), crucially enhanced the premier's control over government (Crawford 2000). The second conclusion is that the Savoie thesis holds in some but not all provinces. The recent book by the Institute of Public Administration of Canada study team on administrative styles in the provinces concludes, in the words of its editors, "The development towards a premier or prime minister centred executive style appears to be much more pronounced in the largest Canadian jurisdictions, with pronounced moves in this direction over the last decade at the federal level and in Ontario, Alberta, and British Columbia. Most of the smaller Canadian provinces retain a system of institutionalized cabinets and Quebec remains the anomaly in also retaining such a style in a large and complex jurisdiction" (Bernier, Brownsey, and Howlett 2005a).

The logic of the previous section, on the contribution to democracy of routinized procedures for cabinet decision making, suggests that central agencies, which facilitate and enforce such procedures, can play a positive role in enhancing democracy. Conversely, though, central agencies are by definition essential to the concentration of power at the centre, a generally undemocratic development in Canadian governance.

Political Staff

Political staff, beyond those in the first minister's office, may constitute the core executive's least examined component. Even studies, such as Savoie's, that delve deeply into the influence of the first minister's political operatives typically give short shrift to the political staff in ministers' offices. Bernier, Brownsey, and Howlett's (2005b) otherwise comprehensive recent volume on the nature and extent of power at the centre at the provincial level devotes almost no attention to ministers' personal, political staff.

Even the most basic information about political staff, such as their numbers, let alone their influence, is not easy to come by. Rapid turnover and vague job titles or descriptions render accurate counting difficult, as do uncertainties as to definitions. What to make of public servants seconded to ministers' offices to perform tasks, such as media relations, that cross the border into the political? How to take into account outside consultants whose fees may not show up in the budget of the minister's office? Clearly, the numbers, roles, and influence of ministers' political staff vary greatly across jurisdictions and, indeed, within jurisdictions depending on the political stripe and outlook of the government party. What is not in doubt, however, is the *potential* for ministerial political staff to exert substantial influence and thus the need to include them in our democratic audit. A separate question, especially in certain provinces, involves the extent and consequences of political appointments to public service positions, but this issue is outside the scope of this study.

Given their explicitly political mandate and orientation, do political staff promote stronger, more direct linkages with the people and serve as a democratic counterweight to the unelected bureaucrats? Or by expediting access to political decision makers for those with party and political connections, do they constitute an undemocratic avenue of influence for a select few? Do ministers' political staff offset or reinforce the concentration of power within the core executive?

158

Framing the issues this way may miss the real democracy-related question about political staff. Do they foster a healthy relationship between the elected politicians and the nonpartisan bureaucrats, thereby making for strong, effective, democratic government? Or do they impede democracy by damaging relations between the political and bureaucratic sides of government? It is fair to add that one person's damaged relations may be the next person's rehabilitated relationship. Our system is premised on a close and respectful association between politicians and bureaucrats but is subverted if the links become too cozy and the essential division between political and bureaucratic tasks is blurred. As well, "close and respectful" does not mean a Sir Humphrey-like bureaucratic manipulation of the elected politicians, as in the TV series *Yes, Minister*. Thus the chief of staff position introduced by the Mulroney government in Ottawa – high-powered, experienced, and well-paid politicos assigned to each minister's office, whose prime function was to counterbalance bureaucratic influence – could be interpreted as redressing an unhealthy imbalance or as imposing harmful barriers between ministers and senior civil servants. The on-the-ground experience with these politicos was mixed, producing both positive and negative changes in the political-bureaucratic linkage. The experiment was abandoned when the Liberals returned to power in 1993 (Savoie 2003, 123-5). Prime Minister Martin reinstated the chief of staff position (with a healthy pay raise above what ministers' executive assistants had been earning under Chrétien), but without the overtones of mistrust toward the bureaucracy.

As their numbers and potential significance have grown over the years, so too has the control over the hiring of political staff exercised by the first minister's office. This varies widely across and within jurisdictions: newly appointed or weak ministers may have key political staff imposed on them from the centre; solid, more established ministers are usually empowered to hire their own staff, subject to a light vetting by the first minister's people; top ministers brook no interference from the first minister's office in staff appointments. Still, it is noteworthy that even though these are the minister's *personal* political staff, the first minister's political operatives play a significant role in their selection. The PMO/Premier's Office is doubtless interested in controlling ministerial political staff and the ministers themselves, if deemed accident-prone. Usually, though, concerns about quality control loom larger. Simply put, the centre worries that ministers, through ignorance, misguided loyalty to faithful but incompetent supporters, or garden-variety bad judgment, will hire subpar staff – a well-founded concern, as the discussion below suggests.

Once political staff are hired, on a day-to-day basis the first minister's office typically exerts little control over them. While information requests and explicit political direction on particular files are common, the PMO/Premier's Office lacks the capacity for routine oversight and management of ministerial staff. Ministers' staff may chafe at interference from the political centre, but the political figures there bemoan their inability to control the staff in ministers' offices. Overall, following the logic about the dangers of concentrated power at the centre, it is probably a good thing for Canadian democracy that the power of the first minister's staff over individual ministers' staffs is relatively limited.

A long-time player in Canadian political backrooms once sagely observed, "In politics, there's often less than meets the eye." This adage clearly applies to ministerial staff. On paper, their power is formidable: they are privy to crucial, confidential information both political and administrative, they control access to the minister, and they are her closest, most trusted advisors. The reality may be very different, in part because the crush of business forces them to concentrate on only a small proportion of the myriad issues facing the minister's department, and in part because they lack experience or ability. One assessment of political staff in Ottawa concluded that "the Canadian system provides a contrasting example of an executive having much more extensive but arguably less effective political staff ... as sources of policy advice political staff in Canada probably rank among the weakest. By and large a typical minister's office tends to be unduly preoccupied with picayune political matters" (Bakvis 1997, 114). A more recent comparative study commented that ministers' executive assistants, the most senior political staffers, hold "a relatively junior position [that] enjoys neither the salary nor the status" of the Mulroney-era chiefs of staff, who themselves were widely seen as not living up to their promise of exercising clout on a par with that of senior mandarins (King 2003, 40). It remains to be seen whether the upgraded chiefs of staff in the Martin government will warrant a different conclusion.

At the provincial and territorial level, an even less charitable assessment is often deserved. In Ottawa, the pay is better, the talent pool larger, and the national stage more alluring; accordingly the political talent tends to be of higher calibre. Of course, some ministers' personal staff in the provinces and territories are bright, knowledgeable, politically astute, and wield extensive influence. Many, however, are young, lack government experience, and have little or no substantive knowledge of their ministers' policy sectors; others are "political hacks" who owe their positions more to loyalty and partisan connections than to talent. Moreover, the turnover in these high-pressure jobs is high, not least because the very best may find themselves lured away to the first minister's office.

All this adds up to a sharply discounted estimate of the actual influence – for democratic good or ill – of ministerial staff, but does little to address whether the influence they do possess enhances or undermines democracy. Given how little we really know about these figures, and the wide variability of their roles and effectiveness, our answer must necessarily be speculative. On balance, ministers' personal political staff can be judged a positive force for democracy, although, as with their overall role and status, much "is a reflection of the minister and his operating framework" (King 2003, 42). The raison d'être for political staff is to assist the minister in carrying out her political functions: gathering information and advice from diverse sources; providing a political complement (or, if necessary, counterweight) to the permanent bureaucracy; providing routine but essential support for the minister's political duties to party, constituency, and region; and – by no means least in democratic terms – ensuring that the minister knows about and takes into account the views of private government members. If they perform these functions well, political staff advance the interests of the minister as elected representative and elected decision maker.

Political staff can of course behave in ways antithetical to democracy, fostering an exclusionary, unrepresentative style of governance that constrains rather than encourages broad-based participation. Inferior political staff can also undercut the effectiveness of elected ministers through erratic or uninformed actions. To the extent that these things occur, though, the fault lies more with the minister than with the staff, in that he has either consciously approved such practices or implicitly accepted them through culpable inattention. Otherwise put, political staff are not inherently undemocratic in nature.

Three subsidiary points may be cited in favour of political staff as net contributors to democracy. First, the rise of personal ministerial staff can, as it has in Britain, usurp the role of the permanent bureaucracy to the point where not only are ministers less professionally served but the attractions of a public service career are palpably lessened (King 2003, 16). An alternative outcome, evident in Australia and New Zealand, may be that growth in the numbers and influence of ministerial staff "has protected the civil service from governments that wish to politicise its upper echelons" (King 2003, 14). The Canadian experience generally seems to promote a healthy division of labour between the political and the administrative, with some notable exceptions at the provincial level. Second, at the federal level at least, political staff foster inclusion, an essential Audit benchmark, by focusing ministerial attention on regional needs and concerns, thereby acting "as a counterbalance to the bureaucracy [which] at times is overly preoccupied with the interests of central Canada" (King 2003, 42). Finally, the straightforward and unabashedly political appointment process for political staff greatly enhances the possibilities for bringing persons from social groups otherwise underrepresented in the upper reaches of government – women, visible minorities, the disabled, Aboriginals – into key positions. Whether this actually happens to any significant extent is an open question, but the potential is substantial.

On the debit side, political staff in Canada do not score well in terms of accountability and transparency. A recent comparative analysis of five Anglo-Celtic Westminster systems found that "special advisers" – personal political staff – are everywhere less subject to regulation and oversight than are elected officials or permanent public servants (King 2003). Ministerial staff are subject to conflict of interest guidelines or legislation in most Canadian jurisdictions, but much more supervision is possible. In Britain a Code of Conduct for Special Advisers "covers matters such as the tasks which special advisers can do, prevention of the use of resources for political party purposes, contact with the media and the holding by advisers of political party office. It also establishes a complaints structure" (King 2003, 15). Yet even in Britain a recent report from the Committee on Standards in Public Life, a prestigious independent advisory agency, recommended strengthening the code and passage of legislation specifying the roles and restrictions of political staff (Committee on Standards in Public Life 2003, ch. 7). Sound advice for Canada.

The Representational Imperative

At first glance, the representational imperative's pervasive influence on the composition and conduct of Canadian cabinets appears to foster undemocratic consequences. Elevating MPs and MLAs to cabinet on the basis of their social characteristics, the regions they represent, the languages they speak, and similar attributes, rather than their abilities, implies that the people are not as well served in the quality of government decisions as they might be were ministers selected purely on talent. Yet our representative democracy is not about choosing the brightest, the most expert, or the most experienced to govern us; it is about choosing those who can best represent the people. (And of course these representatives have call on the experts and the professionals in the permanent public service.) So long as talent and ability remain of central importance in the selection of the inner core of powerful ministers with heavy responsibilities, as is all but universally the case, the deleterious effects for democracy of the representational imperative can be minimized. It may be true, as Chapter 2 quoted William Matheson's observation, that every cabinet contains some "dullards and nonentities" for representational reasons, but they are usually con-signed to lightweight portfolios where they can do little damage, and assigned experienced political and bureaucratic staff with orders to keep them on a short leash.

And while crass political motives constantly swirl just below the surface of the representational imperative, this distinctively Canadian modification to the British cabinet-parliamentary system clearly holds considerable promise for enhancing cabinet democracy. After all, the key democratic benchmark of inclusiveness – a principal theme of the entire Audit – is greatly advanced when the central decision-making body is explicitly constructed with a view to representing important regional, social, and cultural groups. Having spokespeople at the cen-tre of power not only ensures that the interests of the diverse groups composing Canada (or its provinces and territories) are taken into account in government decisions, it enhances democratic legitimacy by reassuring people that they have representatives in the corridors of power. By the same token, however, legitimacy may suffer if people are dismayed when MPs or MLAs are chosen for ministerial office by virtue of their ethnic heritage or sex. .

A similar logic applies to the regional minister system in national politics (as noted in Chapter 2, little in the provinces and territories approximates Ottawa's explicit designation of ministers with control over political patronage in clearly defined regions). By times inefficient and susceptible to unseemly practices, the regional minister system does offer some assurance that regional interests are considered in the distribution of government largesse, such as capital projects, appoint-ments, and procurement decisions. Democracy is certainly not well served when regional political needs, pressed by powerful and single-minded ministers, trump objective, even-handed allocation processes. But since the allocation of government projects, monies, and jobs is inevitably political, it is more equitable and democratic to have repre-sentatives of all regions at the table when the lolly is given out.

If we are concerned about democratic inclusiveness in the core executive, the problem is less that the representational imperative perverts good and democratic government (save perhaps the worst excesses of regional ministers) as that its influence is limited. The range of groups seen as entitled to ministerial representation is narrow and excludes many social groupings much in need of access to cabinet. Region, ethnicity, linguistic community, culture, sex, and (in qualified ways) religion and occupation are the principal axes for plotting the representational imperative. Economic status, age, sexual orientation, and disability are largely or entirely overlooked when representational considerations are factored into cabinet appointments. By definition, the poor and unemployed have no cabinet representative. And the validity of representation lies very much in the eye of the beholder: modern Canadian cabinets typically contain some ministers from visible minorities, but do Muslims see a Sikh minister as their representative? Are Canadians of Tamil or Somali heritage represented by a minister of Caribbean extraction? The representative imperative may not be all that representative for some social groupings.

The other shortcoming of the representational imperative lies in its uncertain influence behind closed cabinet doors. It is all well and good to appoint ministers on the basis of the social groups they represent, but do they really wield any influence on behalf of those groups? Certainly ministers who serve as little more than window dressing to appease groups or regions – holding insignificant portfolios, sitting on unimportant committees, and enjoying minimal political clout – do little to advance genuine cabinet inclusiveness. More generally, the mere fact that ministers share social characteristics with important groups or interests (even if this was the basis for their cabinet appointments) by no means guarantees that the ministers will indeed speak up for these groups or interests, or that if they do they'll be taken seriously or exercise real influence.

In sum, by promoting inclusiveness in cabinet processes, the representational imperative does contribute to democracy. Still, inclusion of social groups through cabinet representation is uneven, and the effectiveness of ministers' representational efforts variable.

Executive Federalism

With Jennifer Smith's volume for the Democratic Audit, *Federalism* (2004), having so thoroughly puzzled out the complex relationship between federalism and democracy in Canada, this book need not rehash her analysis. One important facet of our exploration of Canadian core executives does, however, entail a brief foray into the Byzantine world of intergovernmental relations: executive federalism.

"Executive federalism" denotes a defining characteristic of Canadian federalism, itself a defining characteristic of governance in this country. The term highlights the extent to which intergovernmental conflicts are resolved, policies developed, agreements struck, and financial transfers sorted out at the executive level, among ministers and senior bureaucrats. Executive federalism primarily refers to intergovernmental bargaining – almost invariably conducted in private – with less concern for the formal niceties of jurisdictional boundaries than for political accommodation.

Solid arguments can be mounted to support the proposition that in the abstract federalism carries substantial democratic potential, but the practical implications of executive federalism in Canada are all but uniformly undemocratic (Smith 2004). More than two decades ago, political scientist Donald Smiley, who coined the term, succinctly yet devastatingly put the case for the baneful influence on executive federalism on Canadian democracy:

> My charges against executive federalism are these:
> First, it contributes to undue secrecy in the conduct of the public's business.
> Second, it contributes to an unduly low level of citizen participation in public affairs.
> Third, it weakens and dilutes the accountability of governments to their legislatures and to the wider public (quoted in Simeon and Cameron 2002, 278).

Various attempts have been made since Smiley wrote to overlay executive federalism with some democratic practices, for example through citizen engagement and consultation processes and through the plebiscite that effectively scuppered the Charlottetown constitutional accord in 1992. Overall, though, Smiley's critique remains valid today.

In addition to Smiley's arguments about the generally undemocratic nature of executive federalism, two points specific to the operation and the powers of the core executive reinforce this judgment. The first relates to the consequences of the increasingly dominant role of central agencies in executive federalism. As the mechanisms of intergovernmental relations have become more sophisticated and as the stakes have grown, the locus of bureaucratic power in federal-provincial-territorial decision making has shifted. Where once negotiations were carried out primarily at the sectoral level – federal health officials dealing with provincial health officials, Ottawa's transportation bureaucrats sorting out problems with their territorial counterparts – central agency officials have taken over as the principal bureaucratic players in much intergovernmental negotiation, especially high-profile, high-stakes matters. This transformation has far-reaching implications for the substance of intergovernmental decisions. The sorts of agreements reached by policy experts from line departments, who tend to share professional norms, long-standing personal relationships, and policy objectives, can be very different from agreements struck by central agency bureaucrats who are primarily concerned with process and with advancing the interests of their governments and have limited familiarity with or attachment to the actual substance of policy (Dupré 1985). Portentous as this may be in policy terms, it has little bearing on democratic concerns. What is of moment in democratic terms, though, is how this development has intensified the concentration of bureaucratic power in the central agencies, which as discussed above are not normally net contributors to democracy.

The second point is the political analogue of the first. Great swaths of policy are determined as much in intergovernmental bargaining sessions as at the cabinet tables in Ottawa and the provincial and territorial capitals. Typically the main actors are the first ministers, the relevant sectoral ministers, and central agency bureaucrats. Ministers other than those directly involved are often effectively excluded. Hiving off significant decision-making authority in this way clearly detracts from cabinet's capacity to engage in collective, collegial – which is to say democratic – decisions, in which all ministers participate.

As was evident in Chapter 4, governments in the Western provinces are less inhibited about experimenting with cabinet structures and processes than their Eastern counterparts are. In this vein a recent innovation with potentially significant implications for executive federalism took the form of a joint meeting of the Alberta and BC cabinets. It is premature to judge whether institutionalization of this practice might hold positive or negative consequences for democracy. Much turns on the question of whether this meeting was essentially an empty public relations gimmick or a genuine decision-making exercise. The predictably anodyne pre- and postmeeting press releases offered little insight; nor did media coverage, which focused on how the provinces' alliance would affect relations with Ottawa (Government of Alberta/Government of British Columbia 2003a; 2003b; Olsen 2003).

Institutions Matter

This chapter has demonstrated that even apparently mundane structural and procedural elements of the core executive may have important implications for the health of Canadian democracy. Most of the organizational features examined in this chapter contain possibilities for both enhancing and undermining Canadian democracy, and our analysis of them proceeds more on the basis of informed speculation than on hard empirical evidence. For example, an in-depth study of ministers' political staff might refute our rather tentative conclusion that overall they are net contributors to democracy in this country.

With that caveat, we can advance the proposition that several key organizational features of Canadian cabinets and core executives either enhance or hold substantial capacity to enhance the quality of democracy in this country: the representational imperative, cabinet committee systems, bureaucratized cabinet procedures, and ministers' personal political staff. On balance, the growth of central agencies probably diminishes democracy and the practice of executive federalism almost certainly does so. Other factors, such as the size of cabinet and whether it is organized into formal tiers, affect democracy only to a very limited extent if at all.

The machinery at the centre of government is ever changing. This chapter demonstrates that while reforms to the structures and processes of the core executive may enhance or diminish democracy, definite promise exists for advancing democracy by modifying organizational forms. Some especially promising avenues are explored in the concluding chapter.

Chapter 5

Strengths

- More and better opportunities for a wider range of ministers to partici-pate effectively in cabinet decision making are offered by larger, single-tiered cabinets and, on balance, extensive and active cabinet committee systems.

- Standardized procedures for cabinet decisions, enforced by central agencies, promote orderly, well-informed decisions.

- Political staff can significantly assist ministers in fulfilling their roles as elected representatives and elected decision makers.

- Ensuring that as many regions and groups as possible are represented around the cabinet table promotes inclusive cabinet decision making.

Weaknesses

- Larger cabinets tend to enhance the first minister's influence. Tiered cabinets, with relatively small inner cabinets, concentrate power in a few hands.

- Extensive recourse to cabinet committees excludes ministers from important decisions.

- Extensive bureaucratization of cabinet decision making opens the door for appointed officials, especially those in central agencies, to usurp the power of elected ministers.

- Political staff can foster an exclusionary, unrepresentative style of governance.

- Appointing ministers on the basis of their social characteristics rather than on the basis of talent and ability undercuts cabinet effectiveness.

- Executive federalism promotes the concentration of power among a small number of elected and appointed officials, renders government decision making more opaque than it needs to be, and dilutes accountability.

6

DEMOCRACY IN THE ELECTED DICTATORSHIP?

Canadian cabinets, first ministers, and the other elements of the core executive are integral elements of our representative democracy. As has been repeatedly demonstrated in this book, the core executive can be organized and can operate in many different ways without offending the essential constitutional principles of the Westminster system. Thus the variations evident in the core executive across Canada, and indeed across the Anglo-Celtic world (as well as those that remain in the realm of possibility), hold great potential for affecting democracy in this country – for good and ill.

Those in the core executive can certainly behave in ways inimical to democracy. Concentrating enormous power in a very small number of people can severely limit the capacity of elected representatives to participate in key decision-making processes. Concentration can also foster governance that is secretive, exclusionary, and unaccountable. Yet so too first ministers, cabinets, and those around them can pay genuine heed to the democratic norms suffusing our political system, operating in ways that enhance participation, representation, inclusiveness, transparency, and accountability.

The aim of this book has been to investigate Canadian core executives with a view to finding where the balance lies: is the core executive so undemocratic in its operation and influence as to undermine

Canada's claim to being democratic? Beyond its basic status as the pinnacle of our representative democracy, what elements of democracy can be discerned in the core executive? Overall, in terms of the Canadian core executive, is democracy declining or strengthening? This chapter reviews the answers to these questions and suggests ways of enhancing Canadian democracy through reform of the structure and operation of the core executive.

Advance or Decline?

The principal audit findings are summarized at the ends of the chapters and need not be repeated here. That most of the positive signs noted in chapters 3, 4, and 5 are of recent provenance is in itself an important answer to the question, "Are things getting better or worse?" Consideration of developments in the larger political-governmental context in which the core executive operates points in a similar direction, though negative changes are also evident.

Savoie (1999), Simpson (2001), and others correctly highlight substantial changes in governmental structure and in political practices that work to enhance the power of the first minister. Central agencies, most notably the Prime Minister's Office and the Privy Council Office and their provincial and territorial equivalents, have expanded greatly in both numbers and influence. Long-serving first ministers have historically been the Canadian norm, but in recent decades ministers have become notably more transient, in that they are shuffled frequently during relatively short cabinet careers. This puts the first minister in a stronger position vis-à-vis cabinet colleagues. The trend in political parties toward ever more broadly based leadership selection processes has substantially reduced first ministers' vulnerability to cabinet or caucus revolts. The personality focus of the electronic media intensifies the identification of the government with the first minister, also heightening the first minister's importance.

Yet the magnitude of other, countervailing developments raises the possibility that enhancements to the political-bureaucratic apparatus at the centre may have enabled the first minister only to avoid a decline in influence. Even with recent retrenchments, the state – national, provincial, and territorial versions – is far larger than it was barely a few decades ago, with the range and number of issues competing for core executive attention correspondingly greater. The policy process has grown enormously more complex, and thereby more difficult to control. Over the same period new sources of politically threatening information have become available to the press, which has grown more intrusive and aggressive. The public is less deferential, more cynical, and more demanding. The Charter restricts governments' – and hence core executives' – room to manoeuvre. The capacity of governments at all levels (and again, core executives) has been constrained by a constricting web of domestic intergovernmental arrangements, international economic agreements and agencies, burgeoning transnational corporations and interest groups, and the like.

Of course the overall power of the core executive could be declining even as that power is increasingly concentrated at the centre, and especially in the person of the first minister and his or her key advisors. Chapter 3 suggests that this has occurred to some degree but also that sweeping judgments about autocratic first ministers call for careful and skeptical evaluation.

Principles Underlying Reform

Before turning to specific reform proposals, we should enumerate several principles that both sustain and restrict possibilities for democratizing the Canadian core executive.

First, international comparisons are instructive and suggest structural and procedural innovations of potential value for advancing democracy in Canadian core executives. Yet even within the confines of the Anglo-Celtic Westminster world, institutional transfer can be problematic. Political culture, institutional setting, and political context all affect the success of imported organizational forms and processes. Accordingly, while promising ideas from Australia, Ireland, New Zealand, and the United Kingdom are certainly worth pursuing, the richest source for workable reforms is domestic. Canada's fourteen Westminster systems form a natural laboratory for institutional experimentation, and the successful experiments probably stand a better chance of taking root and flowering when they are transplanted only across the street (as it were) rather than across the ocean.

Second, Canadian governments are complex, multifaceted institutions, so that the advance of democracy within one element – the core executive – is closely tied to developments in other components of the system. For example, it could be argued that the surest means of achieving significant democratic reform of core executives in Canada is the adoption of a new electoral system, such as proportional representation. Similarly, extensive reform of Canadian legislatures (including the establishment of an elected Senate), could have far-reaching consequences for the operations of the country's cabinets, including their democratic elements.

Third, although the Westminster system, especially in Ottawa, is often understandably seen as hidebound, inflexible, and confiningly orthodox, it is in fact anything but. Indeed, the hallmark of British-style responsible government is its flexibility and adaptability. This is evident from even a cursory review of the institutional forms mentioned in this book that are perfectly compatible with the essential principles of responsible government: the consensus governments of Nunavut and the Northwest Territories; the caucus committees of Alberta and British Columbia; Australia's community cabinets; the hybrid executive in Wales; and the tiered cabinets of Britain and Australia.

Fourth, successful democratic reforms rarely ensue from purely structural change: also critical are attitudinal shifts, most notably commitment to genuine democratization. Similarly, positive attitudes can go only so far without a facilitative institutional framework. In other words, progress in democratizing Canadian core executives entails both structural and attitudinal change.

Finally, real change is possible. This claim might seem to overlook the primal political reality that only very rarely do those with power willingly give it up. Beyond accidents or long-term developments, such as increasing influence of competing levels of government, those in power – most notably the first minister and the cabinet – would have to accept and implement the changes that would curtail their power. But this fact does not preclude real change. The key lies less with those who hold power than with those who hope to hold power. If opposition politicians (at least those with realistic prospects of electoral victory) commit to significant reforms *while in opposition* and can be made to deliver on their pledges should they attain office, change is indeed possible. Alternatively, a leadership hopeful in a governing party might take up the cause of serious reform and follow through should he or she emerge victorious in the race to succeed a retiring first minister.

Jeffrey Simpson has written, "In Canada's all-powerful prime-ministerial system, the discretion to call an election when it suits the prime minister is arguably the most precious political advantage of all. No incumbent would dream of yielding such an advantage" (Simpson 2001, 30). He is quite correct. Opposition politicians, however, who daily suffer the indignities of undemocratic institutions, may well dream just such a dream. In British Columbia, Liberal leader Gordon Campbell promised, while in opposition, to give up the power to call elections. Upon his election, he did precisely that, naming the date for the next BC election and introducing a government bill, which was quickly passed, amending the province's Constitution Act to provide for fixed elections. In a similar vein, when he was leader of the Opposition (and enjoying a promising lead in the polls, which held up through the 2003 election) Ontario premier Dalton McGuinty committed himself publicly to a sweeping "Democratic Charter for Ontario," including fixed election dates to eliminate, in his words, "the divine right of premiers to decide when an election will be called" (Ontario Liberal Party 2001). Like their BC counterparts, the Ontario Liberals quickly moved to realize their commitment. (Both Campbell and McGuinty also committed themselves while in opposition to a potentially far more profound change: consultation processes leading to referenda on alternatives to the first-past-the-post electoral system.)

Election of a new government may not be necessary if leadership candidates within the governing party champion serious reform. While running for the Liberal leadership after leaving cabinet, Paul Martin joined the ranks of those concerned about the concentration of power in the Prime Minister's Office by making action on dealing with the so-called democratic deficit through parliamentary reform a central plank in his platform (Martin 2002-3). Once in office, Martin clearly signalled his commitment to following through on reform promises: the press statements released on his swearing-in emphasized how he "has made democratic reform a top priority," detailing specific initiatives to strengthen Parliament and to enhance the role of parliamentary secretaries within cabinet processes (Office of the Prime Minister 2003; for an analysis of Martin's reform agenda, see Aucoin and Turnbull 2003).

Reform Recommendations

What follow are recommendations for enhancing democracy both within the Canadian core executive and in terms of its position within government. Contextual factors specific to each jurisdiction would determine how effective each proposed reform might be as well as possible difficulties in bringing it about. In some jurisdictions, the suggested reforms are already in place. All are feasible and practical. None offend the fundamental principles of responsible government. Few entail significant financial cost.

STRENGTHENING PARLIAMENT AND THE PROVINCIAL/ TERRITORIAL LEGISLATURES

The first reform aimed at advancing democracy at the level of the core executive relates primarily to a subject only tangentially discussed in this book: Parliament. Yet in terms of both changing politicians' atti-tudes toward the extent and nature of core executive power and devel-oping formal processes to restrain it and hold it accountable, many of the most feasible changes lie in the parliamentary realm.

With David Docherty's contribution to the Democratic Audit project, *Legislatures* (2004), setting out in detail the possibilities and prospects for reforming Canada's legislative institutions, there is no need here to elaborate ways in which Parliament and the provincial and territorial legislatures might be strengthened. Larger Houses, more muscular committees, enhanced services and supports for elected members, more independence of action by members (implying not only tolerance from the core executive, but also willingness on members' parts to act independently), greater respect for the institution of Parliament, and other reforms would all contribute to enhancing core executive democ-racy. Indeed, any strengthening of Canadian legislatures would advance democracy, both in general terms and with specific reference to the core executive.

FIXED ELECTION DATES

As mentioned above, holding elections at fixed intervals is a straight-forward and easily accomplished reform, requiring only passage of a short bill, provided the political will exists. British Columbia did just that, and in Ontario, the McGuinty Liberals brought forward legislation early in their mandate. Federally, Conservative Party leader Stephen Harper called for fixed elections in the party's 2004 election platform (Conservative Party of Canada 2004). For some, the essential rationale lies in removing the unfair advantage enjoyed by an incumbent gov-ernment to call an election at a time most conducive to its re-election prospects. Others see it more as a way to curtail first ministers' capac-ity to bully their caucuses by threatening balky MPs or MLAs with an election should they refuse to fall into line (for an instance of a first minister doing just that, see MacKinnon 2003, 123-4). Either way, the result is a palpable diminution of the first minister's power.

Critics sometimes accuse proponents of fixed election dates of wanting to Americanize Canadian politics by abandoning a central tenet of responsible government. Such was the critique launched by the Ontario Tories against the McGuinty Liberals' promise of fixed elections in the province's most recent election. It is thus important to clarify that legislated election dates would be subject to the responsible government requirement that the government retain the confidence of the House. Loss of a vote of confidence would entail the usual consequences – typically an election, though possibly formation of a new government under a new first minister – overriding any legislated provision specifying the length of the parliamentary term.

Involving Private Government Members in Cabinet Processes

Involving members of the government caucus in cabinet processes probably rates as the most far-reaching and controversial reform proposal. That some would see the idea of permitting elected MPs and MLAs access to cabinet documents and according them a modicum of influence over cabinet decisions as radical and inappropriate speaks volumes about the need to empower legislators and to open cabinet processes to a greater number of the people's representatives. This step need not, and almost certainly would not, entail any fundamental reordering of power relations. The most powerful players in the core executive – the first minister and his or her key advisors, both elected (cabinet) and unelected – would remain the most powerful players. Still, enabling a wider range of elected representatives to participate could render cabinet decision making more inclusive and democratic.

Canadian experience offers several possible methods for enhancing the involvement and influence of private government members in cabinet processes. The least extreme would see the chief government whip or caucus chair take part in cabinet discussions with an explicit mandate to bring the views of government backbenchers forward. (This assumes that the whip or caucus chair has no portfolio responsibilities that could detract from his or her capacity to speak on behalf of back-benchers and that on some issues would constitute a conflict of inter-est.) A better alternative would be for actual backbenchers to sit in on cabinet meetings as caucus representatives, perhaps on the rotational model followed in Saskatchewan.

Every government caucus has some role in the policy process, though mostly it is very limited, perhaps little more than hearing what cabinet has decided before the public is informed. Moreover, processes for caucus involvement are usually inconsistent and ad hoc; for exam-ple, caucus normally receives little advance notice of topics to be dis-cussed and few substantive documents. Accordingly, the clout exercised by Canadian caucuses tends to be sporadic as well as meagre. Various concrete examples demonstrate, however, that it is not only possible but beneficial to involve the government caucus in cabinet decision making routinely. Former Saskatchewan finance minister Janice Mac-Kinnon, for example, writes enthusiastically of the political and policy dividends accruing from seriously involving the government caucus in budgetary as well as legislative decisions (MacKinnon 2003). Typically, formal caucus involvement in the policy process is restricted to draft legislation, but it could be extended to nonlegislative initiatives.

Aside from the distinctive structures and processes of consensus government in Nunavut and the Northwest Territories, which are scarcely likely to be adopted "south of sixty," the most radical method yet devised in Canada for involving private government members in cabinet processes is the caucus committee favoured in Alberta, British Columbia, and most recently, Ontario. A much more intensive examina-tion of this intriguing development than was possible in Chapter 4 would be needed before any definitive judgments could be tendered as to the access these bodies enjoy and the influence they wield, but their possibilities are substantial. As to the objection that coopting govern-ment backbenchers into cabinet processes keeps them under control and uncritical, given the quiescence of the typical Canadian govern-ment backbencher, this is not much of a loss.

Another potential objection to private members' service on cabinet committees and their attendance at cabinet, or to caucus review of draft legislation, may readily be discounted. In the admittedly limited Canadian experience, leaks of confidential or sensitive information from government backbenchers simply have not been a problem. Janice MacKinnon writes that involving the government caucus in every major budget decision "paid huge dividends" with no leaks whatsoever (MacKinnon 2003, 105). Involving private government members in cabinet processes poses no threat to cabinet secrecy.

The enhanced roles given parliamentary secretaries by Prime Minister Martin, featuring greater policy responsibility, a measure of access to cabinet and cabinet committees, and status as privy councillors, could be construed as expanding the influence of private government members. The change is probably better understood as an expansion of cabinet through the addition of a tier of (very) junior ministers. Still, assuming that the reality of this initiative approximates its promise, the net result is a more inclusive and participatory core executive.

RESTRICTING MINISTERIAL OFFICE TO EXPERIENCED PARLIAMENTARIANS

Canadian cabinets are hardly awash in ministers without legislative seats. Moreover, constitutional convention requires nonparliamentarians who are appointed as ministers to obtain elected (or senatorial) office. Nevertheless, nonparliamentarians serve as ministers more often in Canada than in other Westminster systems, where the practice either is proscribed by law or contravenes deeply ingrained norms. Even the relatively short periods of time during which extraparliamentary ministers wield power constitute an affront to parliamentary democracy.

If first ministers think that their caucuses lack either talent or persons with the requisite social characteristics, by all means let them look beyond the ranks of their backbenchers for ministers. Such appointments, however, should follow rather than precede the acquisition of a legislative seat. Otherwise put, as in New Zealand and Ireland, ministers should be legally required to hold parliamentary office. This would not require a formal constitutional amendment; simply passing a short bill through Parliament or the provincial or territorial legislature would do the trick.

Another, related reform would be more difficult to implement, for it would reverse long-standing informal norms: ending the distinctively Canadian practice of appointing vast numbers of ministers lacking even minimal parliamentary experience. Leaving aside the question of whether experienced legislators make better (or at least less error-prone) ministers, for ministers to understand and respect parliamentary democracy, surely it is reasonable to expect them to have lived the life of a private member. Such a requirement could be problematic in small provincial houses, which are subject to extensive turnover. Perhaps, however, the problem is not that the goal is impractical, but that provincial legislatures are too small.

EXPANDING ACCESS TO CABINET DOCUMENTS THROUGH FOI

Cabinets simply could not engage in the frank discussions essential to good decision making, nor could ministers make the tough decisions they are called upon to render, without cabinet secrecy. Openness and transparency are admirable and democratic features, appropriate in many areas of governmental activity, but cabinet deliberations are not among them.

Yet although the case is weak for public access to records detailing who said what in cabinet or cabinet committee, save in the long term (fifteen to thirty years) or in highly unusual instances such as the Walkerton inquiry, we need not accept that everything to do with cabinet must be shrouded in secrecy. Many cabinet documents, or parts of them, do not require the same strict confidentiality as do accounts of cabinet debates. The discussion in Chapter 4 of how Canadian freedom of information regimes treat cabinet documents only touched the surface of an exceedingly complex and controversial set of issues. It was nonetheless clear that considerable scope exists for expanding public access to certain types or components of cabinet documents, and that this could be accomplished without harm to the essential principle of cabinet secrecy. The provisions of the Nova Scotia FOI legislation and ideas put forward in various reports of the federal information commissioner suggest directions for reform. The fundamental principles of cabinet secrecy and cabinet solidarity are not likely to be compromised by less stringent restrictions on severing and disclosing background material given to ministers or by easing the exemptions on material relating to cabinet decisions that have already been implemented.

Indeed, a former senior PCO official argues that the centrally important responsible government principle of cabinet secrecy would be better served by easier access to factual cabinet background documents. Especially at the federal level, legal restrictions on access to such documents, he maintains, is both unwarranted and unwise: "Preventing the disclosure of facts does not conform to the purpose of the cabinet secrecy convention. Moreover, the breadth of these statutory provisions is undermining the legitimacy of the convention" (d'Ombrain 2004, 352).

INSTITUTIONALIZING CABINET TOURS

Cabinet ministers are professional politicians whose gainful employment depends on successfully keeping in contact with their electors. For the most part, though, this relationship entails the minister's role as constituency representative rather than as cabinet member. And while the typical minister is besieged by requests for meetings with all manner of interest groups and supplicants, the people and organizations who typically get to meet the minister are not at all representative of the public. The horrendous demands on ministers' time and the vast number of people desirous of an opportunity to address ministers individually, or cabinet collectively, mean that no practical way exists to ensure anything like unfettered and unskewed public access to cabinet.

Institutionalizing cabinet tours, perhaps on the Australian community cabinet model, is no panacea. Tours may be impractical at the national level, but they could connect provincial and territorial cabinets to the people both substantively and symbolically. Bringing the cabinet (not just individual ministers) to local communities is a far more effective manner of fashioning at least minimal public access to cabinet than formal deputations. That such exercises would entail not just passive cabinet endurance of the public's complaints and entreaties but also extensive promotion of the government's views and policies should make them politically attractive to cabinets and first ministers.

Several issues would need to be realistically assessed: how often cabinet tours or public meetings might take place; the extent to which the usual suspects – organized interest groups and veteran political activists – might dominate the process; the prospects that such public encounters might actually affect policy making; and of course the costs (reckoned in terms of money, logistical requirements, and ministers' and officials' time). Still, this is a reform worth pursuing.

So too, an idea floated during Paul Martin's bid for the Liberal Party leadership that seems to have fallen by the wayside is worth revisiting. Key Martin supporter Ralph Goodale (who subsequently became Martin's finance minister) told the media that the prime minister-in-waiting was considering a "mobile PMO" – "leaving Ottawa on a regular basis to work in the regions, and holding cabinet meetings outside of the nation's capital" (Taber 2003). Since coming to office, beyond holding a cabinet meeting in Kelowna, British Columbia, Prime Minister Martin has been silent on this possibility, but it bears consideration.

Strengthening Accountability of Ministerial Staff

As this chapter was being written, the offices of two senior ministerial staff in British Columbia were raided by the police in connection with a drug and money-laundering operation, with possible influence-peddling implications, and many boxes of documents were carted off. No charges were laid, at least initially, but one staffer was fired and another was suspended with pay. Although the specifics, and the final resolution, are not germane here, the incident highlights an important and much-needed democratic reform of the core executive. Ministerial staff – including the political operatives in the PMO and its provincial and territorial equivalents – occupy strategic positions within the core executive and often exercise great influence. Yet as a rule they are not subject to the same stringent conflict of interest provisions and accountability mechanisms that govern the activities of ministers and senior bureaucrats. Political staff are typically covered by ethical and legal guidelines, but without the same degree of scrutiny and sanction as other members of the core executive. As the Wickes Commission in the UK has argued, ministerial political staff should be subject to the same standards of ethical behaviour and accountability as are ministers, deputy ministers, and other powerful members of the core executive (Committee on Standards in Public Life 2003).

Enhancing Caucus Control of Party Leaders

Party leadership selection processes go a long way toward explaining why Canadian first ministers are more powerful than their counterparts in other Anglo-Celtic Westminster systems. The cases of Stockwell Day and (perhaps) Jean Chrétien may be cited as evidence that Canadian party leaders are not secure from being forced out of office by their caucuses. But by comparison with the all-but-instantaneous and final ousters of party leaders such as Margaret Thatcher and Iain Duncan Smith in the UK and Bob Hawke in Australia, the Canadian affairs were uncertain and drawn out. On balance, as the data in Chapter 3 demonstrate, Canadian party leaders, and especially first ministers, need have little fear of the kind of cabinet or caucus revolts that oust sitting first ministers elsewhere. The root cause is not hard to find: formal mechanisms for selecting and deposing party leaders in this country almost invariably encompass conventions or partywide elections but make no provision for caucus action. Not only does the parliamentary party lack the procedural means for removing the leader, it also lacks the moral authority to reverse a decision taken by the party as a whole.

Even if parties accepted the wisdom of according their parliamentary caucuses the capacity to remove leaders or at least trigger leadership reviews – a large "if" indeed, smacking as it does of elitism and disdain for democratic processes – implementing such a reform could be difficult. Political parties are private organizations; control of internal matters, including leadership selection and review processes, largely rests in their hands and is generally not subject to governmental regulation. In other words, unlike the other reforms proposed in this chapter, a government cannot impose this modification by legislation or through control of core executive machinery.

Still, the first minister's practically unassailable position contributes significantly to the concentration of power at the centre. This enhancement of the first minister's power needs to be reduced by empowering the government caucus with a formal mechanism for challenging the first minister's leadership. Neither leaders nor rank and file members in any party are likely to countenance giving the caucus authority to depose a leader altogether. A reasonable measure, which would retain the party members' ultimate power to choose and dismiss leaders while lessening the first minister's domination of the parliamentary party, would entail a majority caucus vote triggering a formal leadership review. Whether this should involve a secret ballot or an open vote is a difficult question.

This change would hardly enfeeble first ministers – no one worries about weak first ministers in Britain, Australia, and New Zealand, where parliamentary parties do depose party leaders. Indeed, opposition leaders would probably be more affected than first ministers. Increased accountability to caucus would nonetheless go some distance toward redressing the imbalance of power within and around the core executive.

Reducing Party Leaders' Control over Nominations and Constituency Organizations

Some minor aspects of party operations, which contribute to party leaders' powers, are subject to legislative regulation. The scope for constraining the clout of party leaders (especially first ministers) in this way is limited, but even minor advances are worth pursuing. Certainly, parties must have control over who carries the party label into elections and over key activities of local constituency organizations. Yet this control need not be vested in the person of the party leader. Wherever the formal power resides, the party leader will retain extensive authority over such matters. Transferring authority for sanctioning party candidates and disbanding constituency organizations from the leader to the party executive would hardly constitute a profound shift of power, but it would marginally reduce the first minister's control over ministers and MPs or MLAs.

This reform could be realized through legislation, but a related change in the powers of the first minister as party leader could, like granting the caucus the capacity to institute leadership reviews, be accomplished only by amending party constitutions. In a number of Canadian parties, among them the national Liberal Party and the Ontario Liberal Party, the leader may impose his or her favoured candidate on local riding associations. This authority enables the leader to bolster the party's roster of minority candidates, to recruit "star" candidates, and to ride herd on maverick constituency organizations. But it also offends against democratic precepts and enhances the first minister's power, so should be ended.

Remaining Open to New Ideas

The principle was set out earlier in this chapter that the Westminster system is not rigid and fossilized but adaptable and open to new forms and processes. Consequently, objections that proposed reforms offend against the hallowed tenets of responsible government – especially that most lethal of arguments, that a prospective change would Americanize Canadian politics – should not be accepted at face value. Certain principles are indeed inviolate under responsible government, but the mechanisms for realizing them are many and varied.

To be sure, we need to know more about the operations and effectiveness of innovative experiments both in Canada and abroad, such as the caucus committees of Alberta, British Columbia, and Ontario, the hybrid executive in the National Assembly of Wales, and the community cabinets of Australia. And while we must not be naïve about claims as to their efficacy in enhancing democracy, we should not forget that the genius of the Westminster system lies in its adaptability. Pretensions about supposed unchangeable orthodoxy that preclude experimentation are antithetical to the continuing evolution of democracy in this and other Westminster countries. Both freedom of information regimes and proportional representation were initially decried as contravening the essence of British-style responsible government but have been seamlessly adapted into Anglo-Celtic Westminster polities.

Canadian democracy will necessarily remain a work in progress. On the one hand, it is well to be vigilant about such possible threats to democracy as the concentration of power at the centre. On the other hand, we must recall that whatever the attractions of various ideas about direct and deliberative democracy, ours remains a representative democracy in which the first minister, the cabinet, and other important members of the core executive gain and wield power through legitimate democratic processes. Canadian core executives are certain to experience continued changes in their composition, structure, and operation; these changes can and should contribute to the enhancement of Canadian democracy.

Discussion Questions

Chapter 1: The Scope and Criteria for the Audit

1 Canada is essentially a representative democracy, with elements of direct and deliberative democracy mixed in. How realistic is it to expect representative democracy to give way to direct or deliberative democracy in this country?

2 What's the point of referring to the "core executive" rather than to the cabinet?

3 Are the constitutional principles underpinning responsible government essentially flexible or essentially rigid?

4 How convincing are this chapter's arguments that responsible government is democratic?

Chapter 2: Cabinet Government in Canada

1 Does it matter whether the social characteristics of Canadian cabinets mirror the social characteristics of the Canadian population?

2 Should cabinet ministers be selected purely on the basis of merit and ability, or should the representational imperative play a role in cabinet composition?

3 Are the differences in cabinet structure and composition between Canada and other Anglo-Celtic countries of any real significance?

4 What are the principal advantages and disadvantages of consensus government as it operates in Nunavut and the Northwest Territories?

Chapter 3: The First Minister As Autocrat?

1 Has the Canadian cabinet become little more than a focus group for the first minister?

2 What are the most important constraints on the first minister's power? How effective are they?

3 Do Canadian first ministers have too much power?

4 Are Canadian first ministers becoming more or less powerful? Why?

Chapter 4: Public Participation in Cabinet Processes?

1 Is it realistic to expect cabinets and cabinet committees to meet regularly with nongovernmental organizations? If this were to happen, what sort of groups would be likely to have regular access to cabinet and what sort would not?

2 Do cabinet tours and meetings outside the capital have any value beyond government public relations? How could this value be maximized?

3 Is secrecy really essential for cabinet decision making? Can the public gain better access to cabinet documents without compromising effective decision making?

Chapter 5: Democracy through Cabinet Structure and Process?

1 Do central agencies have too much power? As far as enhancing democracy is concerned, are central agencies part of the problem or part of the solution?
2 Would it be better to replace political staff with nonpartisan, permanent public servants?
3 Has the representational imperative outlived its usefulness as a principle of cabinet composition?
4 Can executive federalism be modified to permit greater democracy?

Chapter 6: Democracy in the Elected Dictatorship?

1 Should Canadians be worried about increasing concentration of power at the centre?
2 What lessons should Canadians draw from other countries about how to maximize democracy with respect to the core executive?
3 Are there so many entrenched interests unwilling to give up their existing power that real change cannot occur?
4 What are the most promising ideas for enhancing democracy with respect to the Canadian core executive?

Appendix: Sources of Audit Information

The democratic audit reported in this book made limited use of primary government documents, but is largely based on secondary sources, interviews, and, for certain issues, questionnaires. Most of the interview material draws on my long-term study of provincial cabinets. This project includes approximately 180 personal interviews with ministers, former ministers, central agency bureaucrats, and senior politicos in Nova Scotia, Ontario, Manitoba, and British Columbia. These interviews, conducted on a not-for-attribution basis (save those with first ministers), focused on the formal and informal structures and processes of the core executives in these provinces. Under way since 1990, the project covers the period from the early 1970s to the late 1990s.

In addition, in concert with my colleague David Cameron, I conducted several dozen interviews with Ontario political and bureaucratic figures in researching the 1995 transition in Ontario (Cameron and White 2000); many of these interviews touched directly on elements of the Ontario core executive. As well, I've been researching the governmental institutions of Nunavut and Northwest Territories for the better part of two decades; this work has involved numerous personal interviews with past and present core executive figures. Finally, *Cabinets and first ministers* draws on a number of interviews I conducted in 1986 and 1987 while preparing a study of the Ontario premiership (White 1988). Unattributed quotations are taken from these various sets of interviews.

Since information on such practices as backbench participation in cabinet processes, travel by cabinet, and public access to cabinet documents was fragmentary and often outdated, I sent a structured questionnaire inquiring into these and other topics to the cabinet secretary (or equivalent) in Ottawa and all provinces and territories. The response rate was gratifying; eventually, with some poking and prodding, all fourteen jurisdictions returned completed questionnaires.

Additional Reading

W.A. Matheson's *The prime minister and cabinet* (1976) is now dated but is indispensable for the historical development of the federal cabinet up to the early 1970s. Thomas Hockin's edited collection, *Apex of power: The prime minister and political leadership in Canada* (1977), is also somewhat dated but still contains much of value; among other things it includes Denis Smith's "President and Parliament: The transformation of parliamentary government in Canada." Another useful collection is Leslie Pal and David Taras's *Prime ministers and premiers: Political leadership and public policy in Canada* (1988). Herman Bakvis's *Regional ministers: Power and influence in the Canadian cabinet* (1991) covers more than the title might suggest and is also essential reading.

Beyond framing the debate on undue concentration of power in the prime minister's inner circle, Donald Savoie's influential *Governing from the centre: The concentration of power in Canadian politics* (1999) contains much rich detail and insight into the core executive. Herman Bakvis's "Prime minister and cabinet in Canada: An autocracy in need of reform?" (2001) and Paul Thomas's "Governing from the centre: Reconceptualizing the role of the PM and cabinet" (2003-4) are important critiques of the Savoie thesis. Savoie's more recent *Breaking the bargain: Public servants, ministers, and Parliament* (2003) doesn't advance the earlier book's thesis, but does provide valuable material directly relevant to the core executive.

As is typically the case in Canadian political science, the literature on the federal cabinet is far more extensive than that on provincial cabinets; important exceptions are Christopher Dunn's *The institutionalized cabinet* (1995) and "Premiers and cabinets" in his edited collection, *Provinces* (1996). A new collection edited by Luc Bernier, Keith Brownsey, and Michael Howlett, *Executive styles in Canada: Cabinet structures and leadership practices in Canadian government* (2005b) features chapters on every provincial cabinet.

A classic treatment of the principles of Westminster responsible government is A.H. Birch's *Representative and responsible government* (1969); in the Canadian context, Peter Aucoin, Jennifer Smith, and Geoff Dinsdale's *Responsible government: Clarifying essentials, dispelling myths and exploring change* (2004) combines solid scholarship with hard-headed analysis.

A good many former Canadian ministers have written autobiographies — or at least had them ghostwritten. Some are well worth reading, but few devote much time to the inner workings of government. Notable exceptions are former Saskatchewan finance minister Janice MacKinnon's *Minding the public purse: The fiscal crisis, political trade-offs and Canada's future* (2003) and *No holds barred:*

My life in politics (1997), the memoirs of former federal Tory minister John Crosbie. Similarly, Canadian first ministers' recollections rarely have much to say about cabinet; an outstanding exception is *Political management in Canada* (1998), a polished version of extended conversations between former Saskatchewan premier Allan Blakeney and academic Sandford Borins. Bob Rae's *From protest to power* (1996) and Mike Harcourt's *Mike Harcourt: A measure of defiance* (1996) touch on government decision making. Recent prime ministers have been the subject of numerous biographies, and some provincial premiers, such as Ralph Klein, Bill Vander Zalm, and Frank McKenna, have also been so honoured. The journalists who usually write these books have almost no interest in governmental structures and processes, and thus cabinet and its operations tend to be all but entirely absent from their accounts. Edward Greenspon and Anthony Wilson-Smith's *Double vision: The inside story of the Liberals in power* (1996), however, is a fascinating account of the first years in the troubled relationship between Prime Minister Chrétien and his finance minister, Paul Martin.

Senior cabinet officials tend not to write of their experiences. Two who have are E.E. Stewart, whose *Cabinet government in Ontario: A view from the inside* (1989) offers an insider's perspective on the Davis government of the 1970s and 1980s, and former clerk of the Privy Council Gordon Robertson, whose *Memoirs of a very civil servant: Mackenzie King to Pierre Trudeau* (2000) covers several decades as an Ottawa mandarin.

Among many worthwhile studies of specific aspects of cabinet and core executive are Colin Campbell's "Cabinet committees in Canada: Pressures and dysfunctions stemming from the representational imperative" (1985); Peter Aucoin's "Organizational change in the machinery of Canadian government: From rational management to brokerage politics" (1986), a brilliant analysis of the differing decision-making styles imposed on the core executive by Prime Ministers Trudeau and Mulroney; Micheline Plasse's *Ministerial chiefs of staff in the federal government in 1990: Profiles, recruitment, duties and relations with public servants* (1994); and my own "Shorter measures: The changing ministerial career in Canada" (1998).

The literature on the British cabinet and core executive is extensive and generally of high quality. A good place to start is Simon James's *British cabinet government* (1999). Those seeking more advanced material should consult R.A.W. Rhodes's overview of the massive Whitehall Programme, which produced many publications on the British core executive, "A guide to the ERSC's Whitehall Programme, 1994-1999" (2000). Among the good sources on Australian cabinets are Patrick Weller and Michelle Grattan, *Can ministers cope? Australian federal ministers at work* (1981); James Walter, *The minister's minders: Personal advisors in national government* (1986); Patrick Weller, ed., *Menzies to Keating: The development of the Australian prime ministership* (1992a); Colin Campbell and John

Halligan, *Political leadership in an age of constraint: Bureaucratic politics under Hawke and Keating* (1992); and Glyn Davis, *A government of routines: Executive coordination in an Australian state* (1995). On New Zealand, see Elizabeth McLeay, *The cabinet and political power in New Zealand* (1995).

Two overviews of the academic study of Canadian core executive are Christopher Dunn, "The central executive in Canadian government: Searching for the Holy Grail" (2002), and Evert Lindquist and Graham White, "Analysing Canadian cabinets: Past, present, future" (1997).

Works Cited

Alberta. 1993. Government committees system downsized: Four new standing policy committees announced. News release. 15 January.

Alberta. *Freedom of Information and Protection of Privacy Act.* R.S.A. 2000, c. F25.

Aucoin, Peter. 1986. Organizational change in the machinery of Canadian government: From rational management to brokerage politics. *Canadian Journal of Political Science* 19(1): 3-27.

—. 1999. Prime minister and cabinet: Power at the apex. In *Canadian politics,* ed. James Bickerton and Alain-G. Gagnon, 109-28. 3rd ed. Peterborough, ON: Broadview Press.

Aucoin, Peter, and Herman Bakvis. 1993. Consolidating cabinet portfolios: Australian lessons for Canada. *Canadian Public Administration* 36(3): 392-420.

Aucoin, Peter, Jennifer Smith, and Geoff Dinsdale. 2004. *Responsible government: Clarifying essentials, dispelling myths and exploring change.* Ottawa: Canadian Centre for Management Development.

Aucoin, Peter, and Lori Turnbull. 2003. The democratic deficit: Paul Martin and parliamentary reform. *Canadian Public Administration* 46(4): 427-49.

Axworthy, Thomas. 1988. "Of secretaries to princes." *Canadian Public Administration* 31(2): 247-64.

Babcock v. *Canada (Attorney General),* [2002] S.C.R. 2002, S.C.C. 7.

Bakvis, Herman. 1991. *Regional ministers: Power and influence in the Canadian cabinet.* Toronto: University of Toronto Press.

—. 1997. Advising the executive: Think tanks, consultants, political staff, and kitchen cabinets. In *The hollow crown: Countervailing trends in core executives,* ed. Patrick Weller, Herman Bakvis, and R.A.W. Rhodes, 84-112. New York: St. Martin's Press.

—. 2001. Prime minister and cabinet in Canada: An autocracy in need of reform? *Journal of Canadian Studies* 35: 60-79.

Bakvis, Herman, and Roselle Hryciuk. 1993. An experiment in intrastate federalism: The Cabinet Committee on Canadian Unity. In *Canada: The state of the federation 1993,* ed. Ronald L. Watts and Douglas M. Brown, 117-50. Kingston: Queen's Institute of Intergovernmental Relations.

Bateman, Thomas M.J. 2001. Party democracy increases the leader's power. *Policy Options* (September): 20-3.

Benzie, Robert. 2002. Allies say Harris never discussed teams' tax breaks. *National Post,* 10 October.

Bernier, Luc, Keith Brownsey, and Michael Howlett. 2005a. Modern Canadian governance: Politico-administrative styles and executive organization in Canada. In *Executive styles in Canada: Cabinet structures and leadership practices in Canadian government,* ed. Luc Bernier, Keith Brownsey, and Michael Howlett. Toronto: Institute of Public Administration and University of Toronto Press.

—, eds. 2005b. *Executive styles in Canada: Cabinet structures and leadership practices in Canadian government.* Toronto: Institute of Public Administration and University of Toronto Press.

Birch, A.H. 1969. *Representative and responsible government: An essay on the British Constitution.* Toronto: University of Toronto Press.

Bishop, P., and J. Chalmers. 1999. A response to populism: Community cabinets in Queensland. In *Australasian Political Science Association Conference Proceedings,* 39-46. N.p.

—. 2002. A response to populism: Community cabinets in an Australian state. Unpublished ms.

Blake, Donald. 2001. Electoral democracy in the provinces. *Choices* 7(2): 3-37.

Blakeney, Allan, and Sandford Borins. 1998. *Political management in Canada.* 2nd ed. Toronto: University of Toronto Press.

Bohman, James, and William Rehg. 1997. Introduction. *Deliberative democracy: Essays on reason and politics,* ed. James Bohman and William Rehg. Cambridge, MA: MIT Press.

Bouchard, Benoît. 1999. Address to the Fall 1999 Conference of the Canadian Study of Parliament Group, Ottawa, 26 November.

Brownsey, Keith. 2005. The post-institutionalized cabinet: The administrative style of Alberta. In *Executive styles in Canada: Cabinet structures and leadership practices in Canadian government,* ed. Luc Bernier, Keith Brownsey, and Michael Howlett. Toronto: Institute of Public Administration and University of Toronto Press.

Cameron, David R., Celine Mulhern, and Graham White. 2003. Democracy in Ontario. Paper prepared for the Ontario Panel on the Role of Government. <www.law-lib.utoronto.ca/investing/reports/rp35.pdf> (25 October 2004).

Cameron, David R., and Graham White. 2000. *Cycling into Saigon: The Conservative transition in Ontario.* Vancouver: UBC Press.

Campbell, Colin. 1985. Cabinet committees in Canada: Pressures and dysfunctions stemming from the representational imperative. In *Unlocking the cabinet: Cabinet structures in comparative perspective,* ed. T. Mackie and B. Hogwood, 61-85. London: Sage Publications.

Campbell, Colin, and John Halligan. 1992. *Political leadership in an age of constraint: Bureaucratic politics under Hawke and Keating.* St Leonards, New South Wales: Allen and Unwin.

Canada. *Access to Information Act*. R.S.C. 1985, c. A-1.

Carey v. *Ontario*. [1986] 2 S.C.R.

Chambers, Simone. 2003. Deliberative democratic theory. *Annual Review of Political Science* 6:307-26.

Chrétien, Jean. 1985. *Straight from the heart*. Toronto: Key Porter Books.

Christopherson, David. 2003. Consulting the backbenches: Improving the party caucus in Ontario. *Parliamentarian* 84(2): 147-9.

Committee on Standards in Public Life [UK]. 2003. *Defining the boundaries within the executive: Ministers, special advisers and the permanent civil service*. London: Her Majesty's Stationery Office.

Conservative Party of Canada. 2004. *Demanding better: Conservative Party of Canada, platform 2004*. N.p.: Conservative Party of Canada.

Courtney, John. 2004. *Elections*. Canadian Democratic Audit. Vancouver: UBC Press.

Crawford, Mark. 2000. Co-ordination of communications and policy functions in the B.C. NDP government. Paper presented at the meeting of the British Columbia Political Science Association, University of Victoria, 5-6 May.

Crosbie, John. 1997. *No holds barred: My life in politics*. Toronto: McClelland and Stewart.

Cross, William. 2004. *Political parties*. Canadian Democratic Audit. Vancouver: UBC Press.

Davis, Glyn. 1995. *A government of routines: Executive coordination in an Australian state*. Melbourne: Macmillan Education Australia.

Denver, David. 1998. Britain: Centralized parties with decentralized selection. In *Candidate selection in comparative perspective: The secret garden of politics*, ed. Michael Gallagher and Michael Marsh, 47-71. London: Sage Publications.

De Winter, Lieven. 1991. Parliamentary and party pathways to the cabinet. In *The profession of government minister in Western Europe*, ed. Jean Blondel and Jean-Louis Thiebault, 44-69. New York: St. Martin's Press.

Dicey, A.V. [1885] 1956. *Introduction to the study of the law of the Constitution*, ed. E.C.S. Wade. 9th ed. London: Macmillan.

Docherty, David. 2004. *Legislatures*. Canadian Democratic Audit. Vancouver: UBC Press.

d'Ombrain, Nicholas. 2004. Cabinet secrecy. *Canadian Public Administration* 47(3): 332-59.

Dunn, Christopher. 1995. *The institutionalized cabinet: Governing the western provinces*. Kingston and Montreal: Institute of Public Administration of Canada and McGill-Queen's University Press.

—. 1997. Premier and cabinets. In *Provinces*, ed. C. Dunn, 165-204. Peterborough, ON: Broadview Press.

—. 2002. The central executive in Canadian government: Searching for the Holy Grail. In *The handbook of Canadian public administration,* ed. C. Dunn, 305-40. Don Mills, ON: Oxford University Press.

Dupré, Stephan. 1985. Reflections on the workability of executive federalism. In *Intergovernmental relations,* ed. Richard Simeon, 1-32. Toronto: University of Toronto Press.

Englemann, Frederick C. 1989. Alberta: From one overwhelming majority to another. In *Provincial and territorial legislatures in Canada,* ed. Gary Levy and Graham White, 110-25. Toronto: University of Toronto Press.

Galligan, Yvonne. 1999. Candidate selection. In *How Ireland voted 1997,* ed. Michael Marsh and Paul Mitchell, 57-81. Oxford: Westview Press.

Garr, Allen. 1985. *Tough guy: Bill Bennett and the taking of British Columbia.* Toronto: Key Porter Books.

Glenn, J.E. 1997. Parliamentary assistant: Patronage or apprenticeship? In *Fleming's Canadian legislatures 1997,* ed. Robert J. Fleming and J.E. Glenn, 48-59. Toronto: University of Toronto Press.

Government of Alberta/Government of British Columbia. 2003a. Joint cabinet meeting to build B.C.-Alberta partnership. News release. 6 October.

—. 2003b. Alberta and British Columbia to forge closer bonds. News release. 8 October.

Government of Newfoundland and Labrador. 2001. Ministers meet with the Association of Cultural Industries. News release. 15 June.

Greenspon, Edward, and Anthony Wilson-Smith. 1996. *Double vision: The inside story of the Liberals in power.* Toronto: Doubleday Canada.

Harcourt, Mike, with Wayne Skene. 1996. *Mike Harcourt: A measure of defiance.* Vancouver: Douglas and McIntyre.

Hart, John. 1992. An Australian president? A comparative perspective. In *Menzies to Keating: The development of the Australian prime ministership,* ed. Patrick Weller, 183-201. Melbourne: Melbourne University Press.

Heard, Andrew. 1991. *Canadian constitutional conventions: The marriage of law and politics.* Toronto: Oxford University Press.

Heeney, A.D.P. 1967. Mackenzie King and the cabinet secretariat. *Canadian Public Administration* 10: 366-75.

Hennessy, Peter. 1986. *Cabinet.* London: Basil Blackwell.

Hockin, Thomas A., ed. 1977. *Apex of power: The prime minister and political leadership in Canada.* 2nd ed. Toronto: Prentice-Hall.

Hunt, Wayne. 1995. The prime minister today. In *Politics: Canada,* ed. Paul W. Fox and Graham White, 425-36. 8th ed. Toronto: McGraw-Hill Ryerson.

Information Commissioner of Canada. 2003. *Annual Report, 2002-03.* Ottawa: Information Commissioner of Canada.

James, Simon. 1999. *British cabinet government*. 2nd ed. London: Routledge.

Jennings, Ivor. 1965. *Cabinet government*. 3rd ed. Cambridge: Cambridge University Press.

Johnston, Don. 1986. *Up the hill*. Montreal: Optimum Publishing International.

Jull, Peter. 1991. Canada's Northwest Territories: Constitutional development and Aboriginal rights. In *The challenge of northern regions,* ed. Peter Jull and Sally Roberts, 43-65. Darwin: Australian National University, North Australia Research Unit.

Kermode, David. 2002. Government in the Isle of Man: Tynwald and the Manx Council of Ministers. *Parliamentary Affairs* 55: 682-98.

King, Simon. 2003. *Regulating the behaviour of ministers, special advisers and civil servants*. London: University College London, The Constitution Unit.

Laffin, Martin, and Alys Thomas. 2000. Designing the National Assembly for Wales. *Parliamentary Affairs* 53: 223-33.

—. 2001. New ways of working: Political-official relations in the National Assembly for Wales. *Public Money and Management* 21: 45-52.

Laghi, Brian. 2002. Mulroney says leaders must take good care of caucus. *Globe and Mail,* 20 August, A1.

LeDuc, Lawrence. 2003. *The politics of direct democracy: Referendums in global perspective*. Peterborough, ON: Broadview Press.

Lindquist, Evert, and Graham White. 1997. Analysing Canadian cabinets: Past, present, future. In *New public management and public administration in Canada,* ed. Mohamed Charih and Arthur Daniels, 113-38. Toronto: Institute of Public Administration of Canada.

Lynch, C.J. 1982. The Westminster model in the Pacific. *Parliamentarian* 61: 138-50.

Macaulay, Robert. 2003. *Practice and procedure before administrative tribunals*. Looseleaf. Toronto: Carswell.

McCormick, Peter. 1983. Politics after the landslide: The Progressive Conservative caucus in Alberta. *Parliamentary Government* 4(1): 8-10.

McDonald, Gerard. 2003. The caucus involvement process in the NDP government. In *Inside the pink palace: Ontario legislature internship essays,* ed. Graham White, 281-93. Toronto: Canadian Political Science Association.

Macintosh, John P. 1962. *The British cabinet*. Toronto: University of Toronto Press.

MacKinnon, Janice. 2003. *Minding the public purse: The fiscal crisis, political trade-offs and Canada's future*. Montreal and Kingston: McGill-Queen's University Press.

McLeay, Elizabeth. 1995. *The cabinet and political power in New Zealand*. Auckland: Oxford University Press.

Mallan, Caroline. 2002. Harris blamed for sports tax break. *Toronto Star,* 10 October.

Mallory, J.R. 1956. Cabinet government in the provinces of Canada. *McGill Law Journal* 3: 195-202.

Malloy, Jonathan. 2003. The House of Commons under the Chrétien government. In *How Ottawa spends 2003-04: Regime change and policy shift,* ed. G. Bruce Doern, 59-71. Toronto: Oxford University Press.

Martin, Don. 2002. *King Ralph: The political life and success of Ralph Klein.* Toronto: Key Porter Books.

Martin, Paul. 2002-3. The democratic deficit. *Policy Options,* December-January, 10-12.

Matheson, W.A. 1976. *The prime minister and cabinet.* Toronto: Methuen.

Minister of Environment v. *Information Commission of Canada.* [2003] F.C.A. 68.

Nevitte, Neil. 1996. *The decline of deference: Canadian value change in cross-national perspective.* Peterborough, ON: Broadview Press.

Nova Scotia. *Freedom of Information and Protection of Privacy Act.* S.N.S. 1993, c. 5, as amended by S.N.S. 1999, c. 11.

NWT (Northwest Territories) Legislative Assembly. 2004. *Hansard.*

O'Brien, Kevin. 2003. Some thoughts on consensus government in Nunavut. *Canadian Parliamentary Review* 26(Winter): 6-10.

O'Connor v. *Nova Scotia.* 2001 NSCA 132.

O'Connor, Dennis. 2002. *Report of the Walkerton inquiry.* Part 1. Toronto: Ontario Ministry of the Attorney General.

Office of the Prime Minister. 2003. Democratic reform. News release. 12 December. <http://pm.gc.ca> (25 October 2004).

Olsen, Tom. 2003. B.C., Alberta forge political bond. *Edmonton Journal,* 22 October.

Ontario. *Freedom of Information and Protection of Privacy Act.* R.S.O. 1990, c. F31.

Ontario Information and Privacy Commission. 1993. Order P-514, Appeal P-9200774, Ministry of Consumer and Commercial Relations. 12 August.

Ontario Liberal Party. 2001. McGuinty unveils a democratic charter for Ontario. News release. 9 November.

—. 2003. A real, positive change in how government works. News release. 22 October.

Ontario Management Board of Cabinet. 1989. *Directions.* Toronto: Queen's Printer for Ontario.

Ontario v. *Fineberg.* 1995. Toronto Doc. 220/95 (Div. Ct). 21 December.

Pal, Leslie A., and David Taras, eds. 1988. *Prime ministers and premiers: Political leadership and public policy in Canada.* Toronto: Prentice-Hall.

Palmer, Vaughan. 2001. Open cabinet: A few hits and what's missing. *Vancouver Sun,* 28 June.

—. 2003a. Campbell's "open" cabinet pure infomercial. *Vancouver Sun,* 15 March.

—. 2003b. Tolls and trouble at open cabinet meeting. *Vancouver Sun*, 24 April.

Parliament of Canada. 2003. Ministers named from outside Parliament. 26 June. <www.parl.gc.ca> (25 October 2004).

Plasse, Micheline. 1994. *Ministerial chiefs of staff in the federal government in 1990: Profiles, recruitment, duties and relations with public servants*. Ottawa: Canadian Centre for Management Development.

Privy Council Office. 1998. *Decision-making processes and central agencies in Canada: Federal, provincial and territorial practices*. Ottawa.

—. 2004. *Ethics, responsibility, accountability: An action plan for democratic reform*. Report. 4 February.

Rae, Bob. 1996. *From protest to power*. Toronto: Penguin.

Rhodes, R.A.W. 1995. From prime minister to core executive. In *Prime minister, cabinet and core executive,* ed. R.A.W. Rhodes and Patrick Dunleavy, 11-37. London: Macmillan.

—. 2000. A guide to the ESRC's Whitehall Programme, 1994-1999. *Public Administration* 78(1): 251-82.

Roberts, Alasdair. 1999. Retrenchment and freedom of information: Recent experience under federal, Ontario and British Columbia law. *Canadian Public Administration* 42(Winter): 422-51.

Robertson, Gordon. 2000. *Memoirs of a very civil servant: Mackenzie King to Pierre Trudeau*. Toronto: University of Toronto Press.

Savoie, Donald. 1999. *Governing from the centre: The concentration of power in Canadian politics*. Toronto: University of Toronto Press.

—. 2003. *Breaking the bargain: Public servants, ministers, and Parliament*. Toronto: University of Toronto Press.

—. 2005. The federal government: Revisiting court government in Canada. In *Executive styles in Canada: Cabinet structures and leadership practices in Canadian government,* ed. Luc Bernier, Keith Brownsey, and Michael Howlett. Toronto: Institute of Public Administration and University of Toronto Press.

Schindeler, F.F. 1969. *Responsible government in Ontario*. Toronto: University of Toronto Press.

Seymour-Ure, Colin. 1971. The "disintegration" of cabinet and the neglected question of cabinet reform. *Parliamentary Affairs* 24: 196-207.

Sharp, Mitchell. 1994. *Which reminds me ... A memoir*. Toronto: University of Toronto Press.

Shaw, Marvin E. 1981. *Group dynamics: The psychology of small group behaviour*. 3rd ed. Chicago: Rand McNally.

Simeon, Richard, and David Cameron. 2002. Intergovernmental relations and democracy: An oxymoron if there ever was one? In *Canadian federalism: Performance, effectiveness and legitimacy,* ed. Herman Bakvis and Grace Skogstad, 278-95. Toronto: Oxford University Press.

Simpson, Jeffrey. 2001. *The friendly dictatorship*. Toronto: McClelland and Stewart.

Smallwood v. *Sparling.* [1982]. 2 S.C.R.

Smith, Denis. 1977. President and parliament: The transformation of parliamentary government in Canada. In *Apex of power: The prime minister and political leadership in Canada,* 2nd ed., ed. Thomas A. Hockin, 308-25. Toronto: Prentice-Hall.

Smith, Jennifer. 2004. *Federalism.* Canadian Democratic Audit. Vancouver: UBC Press.

Smith, Martin. 2000. Prime ministers, ministers and civil servants in the core executive. In *Transforming British government.* Vol. 1, *Changing institutions,* ed. R.A.W. Rhodes, 308-25. London: Macmillan.

Speaker, Ray. 1998. Party caucuses behind closed doors. *Canadian Parliamentary Review* 21 (Spring): 4-6.

Speirs, Rosemary. 1986. *Out of the blue: The fall of the Tory dynasty in Ontario.* Toronto: Macmillan of Canada.

Stewart, E.E. 1989. *Cabinet government in Ontario: A view from the inside.* Halifax: Institute for Research on Public Policy.

Taber, Jane. 2003. Martin open to setting up mobile PMO, Goodale says. *Globe and Mail,* 24 July.

Thomas, Paul. 1996. Parties in Parliament: The role of party caucuses. In *Canadian parties in transition,* 2nd ed., ed. A. Brian Tanguay and Alain-G. Gagnon, 221-30. Toronto: Nelson.

—. 1998. *Party caucuses: Behind closed doors.* Occasional paper no. 1. Ottawa: Canadian Study of Parliament Group.

—. 2003-4. Governing from the centre: Reconceptualizing the role of the PM and cabinet. *Policy Options* 25(1): 79-85.

Trudeau, Pierre Elliott. 1993. *Memoirs.* Toronto: McClelland and Stewart.

Urquhart, Ian. 2003a. McGuinty shores up his bench — maybe. *Toronto Star,* 27 October.

—. 2003b. Tories' downfall began at Magna. *Toronto Star,* 27 December.

Walkom, Thomas. 2003. How Eves' empire collapsed. *Toronto Star,* 2 November.

Walter, James. 1986. *The minister's minders: Personal advisors in national government.* Sydney: Oxford University Press.

Weller, Patrick. 1980. Inner cabinets and outer ministers: Some lessons from Australia and Britain. *Canadian Public Administration* 23: 598-615.

—, ed. 1992a. *Menzies to Keating: The Development of the Australian prime ministership.* Melbourne: Melbourne University Press.

—. 1992b. Prime ministers and cabinet. In *Menzies to Keating: The development of the Australian prime ministership,* 5-27. Melbourne: Melbourne University Press.

— 2003. Cabinet government: An elusive ideal? *Public Administration* 81(4): 701-22.

Weller, Patrick, Herman Bakvis, and R.A.W. Rhodes, eds. 1997. *The hollow crown: Countervailing trends in core executives.* New York: St. Martin's Press.

Weller, Patrick, and Michelle Grattan. 1981. *Can ministers cope? Australian federal ministers at work.* Melbourne: Drummond.

Whelan, Eugene, with Rick Archbold. 1986. *Whelan: The man in the green Stetson.* Toronto: Irwin.

White, Graham. 1988. Governing from Queen's Park: The Ontario premiership. In *Prime ministers and premiers: Political leadership and public policy in Canada,* ed. Leslie A. Pal and David Taras, 158-77. Scarborough, ON: Prentice-Hall.

—. 1991. Westminster in the Arctic: The adaptation of British parliamentarism in the Northwest Territories. *Canadian Journal of Political Science* 24 (September): 499-523.

—. 1998. Shorter measures: The changing ministerial career in Canada. *Canadian Public Administration* 41 (Fall): 369-94.

—. 2001. And now for something completely northern: Institutions of governance in the territorial North. *Journal of Canadian Studies* 35 (Winter): 80-99.

—. 2004. Traditional Aboriginal values in a third millennium legislature: The legislative assembly of Nunavut. Paper presented at the International Political Science Association Research Committee of Legislative Specialists Conference on Sub-National Legislatures. Quebec City, 24 October.

Winsor, Hugh. 2002. Tea leaves? Bah: key to PM's plans in civil service. *Globe and Mail,* 1 May, A5.

—. 2003. C-24 a boon to party leaders, not to voters. *Globe and Mail,* 9 June, A5.

Young, Walter D., and J. Terence Morley. 1983. The premier and the cabinet. In *The reins of power: Governing British Columbia,* ed. J. Terence Morley, Norman J. Ruff, Neil A. Swainson, R. Jeremy Wilson, and Walter D. Young, 45-82. Vancouver: Douglas and McIntyre.

Index

A master index to all volumes in the Canadian Democratic Audit series can be found at www.ubcpress.ca/readingroom/audit/index.